DATE

HOBBYCRAFT
AROUND the WORLD

HOBBYCRAFT
AROUND the WORLD

Willard & Elma Waltner

LANTERN PRESS

PUBLISHERS

257 PARK AVENUE SOUTH, NEW YORK 10, N. Y.

© *Copyright 1966 by Lantern Press, Inc.*
All rights reserved.

The following used by permission of Workbasket, copyright by
Modern Handcraft on the dates indicated; From Can to
Canister 1962, Egyptian Jewelry 1964, Lacy Snowflake Doilies 1965,
Corsage Pin-Purse 1965, A Coiled Basket 1965, Oriental Planter for
Plastic Flower Arrangements 1965, Mexican Fiesta String 1965,
Block Printing with Eraser Stamps 1965, Japanese Scroll Painting 1965
The following used by permission of Workbench, copyright by
Modern Handcraft 1957; Marble Roll Game
The following used by permission of Covenant Trails, copyright
by Covenant Press 1964; Penning the Pigs
The following used by permission of Popular Mechanics Magazine, copyright
1963; Go Fly a Kite, including Malay Bow Kite, Floating Hoop Kite.
The following used by permission of Boy's Life, copyright by
Boy Scouts of America on the dates indicated; A Chinese Top—under
the title of "A Flying Saucer" 1965, Horn Bugle 1965, Popcorn
Mosaic 1965, Multiplying Peep Box 1965

Library of Congress Catalog Card Number 66-11074

Published simultaneously in Canada by
George J. McLeod, Limited, Toronto
Manufactured in the United States of America

To Les and Tony
Who became proficient as "Assistant Project Spotters"
when they joined the family.

FOREWORD

Since the earliest recorded history of man there are evidences that "making things" with the hands occupied a great deal of time. At first all implements, all tools and household items were laboriously made by hand through necessity rather than by choice. If families were to have these things to use there was no way to get them except to make them. The skills were taught by each generation to the next.

From earliest times, too, even the items of daily use were decorated by painting, carving or embroidery so that they would be beautiful as well as useful. The type of decoration was typical of the country, and even to the present day the designs have survived as an easily recognizable mark of the locality where they originated.

In our present day machines have taken over the tedious work of producing the many items we need for everyday living. It is no longer necessary to mold bowls, weave cloth, make furniture or carve forks and spoons by hand if we are to have these things. But the desire to make beautiful objects, and the satisfaction of displaying or using those things which we ourselves have made is still inherent in us all. For this reason, the skills of handicraft will probably never die out.

TABLE OF CONTENTS

Chapter 1

LACY SNOWFLAKE DOILIES

The making of lace is an ancient craft, an outgrowth of embroidery. The earliest lace was merely an openwork mesh formed by looping, braiding or twisting threads of cotton, silk, gold, silver or other materials. The name given the early net-like material comes from the Latin word "loquare" which means "making a noose, or snare." We still use the word today though our present day lace is much more intricate in design.

For many years the making of lace was all done by hand. It was hard, slow, and poorly-paid work. It was a craft practiced by whole families in many of the countries of Europe.

Joseph Marie Jacquard was the son of a lace making family of Lyons, France. As he grew up he decided he would not follow the family trade until "The toil should be less wretched and the payment better." So he worked at many different jobs instead, from book binding to hat-making. Still, he never lost interest in the family craft.

When he was nearly fifty years old, in 1801, he heard that the English Society of Arts had offered a prize for the invention of a lace-making machine. He designed one, just to see what he could do with the idea, but did not enter it in the competition. Instead, he put it aside, considering it nothing more than a toy. The whole matter would have been forgotten if a friend, who had seen the machine, had not secretly taken the model to the mayor of Lyons. He, in turn, became so excited by the possibilities of the machine that he reported it to Napoleon. The Emperor was so impressed that he provided funds for the inventor to do further work on the machine, much to the astonishment of that gentleman.

So Jacquard completed his lace-making machine and exhibited it at Lyons. It was immediately smashed by a mob of people who were afraid that if machines came into general use they would put many lace makers out of work. But the idea for the machine was carried to England and through it that country built up a lace-making industry that never died.

In self defense, the French asked Jacquard to rebuild his machine. This he did and was pleased to live to see the day when a great new lace-making trade developed in his own country because of his invention.

Doilies that look something like the net which was first called "lace" can be made in the shape of snowflakes on a simple cardboard loom.

Use heavy, solid cardboard to make the frame. Corrugated cardboard can be used but is not as satisfactory. The size frame shown in the diagram makes a doily that measures 11″ across from point to point. Smaller doilies can also be made on the same frame, but if you want larger ones, increase the size. It can be made any size but the V-notches around the outside edge should always be ½″ apart, and the width of the frame 1″. Cut the notches ⅛″ wide at the top and ⅛″ deep.

Use whatever type of thread you wish for stringing the frame. Fine crochet thread makes an especially lacy doily. Carpet warp is somewhat coarser, and yarn makes a soft, puffy piece.

Wrap the string around the frame, catching it in a notch nearest one of the corners. Tie the string to keep it from slipping.

Take the string across the open part of the frame to the notch next to the corner opposite the starting point. Catch the thread in the notch and pass it around the frame to the under side, across the open part back to the starting point. Bring the thread around to the top of the frame again, catching it in the starting notch, across the frame to the notch opposite, around the frame and back to the starting point once more. There will now be four threads together across the open center portion of the frame. Holding it in the first notch to keep it from slipping out, pass the thread to the second notch, from front to back of the frame. Pass the thread across the frame on the under side and catch it in the notch opposite. Bring it around the frame on top and back to the second notch on the starting side. Continue the winding for another turn. Move the thread to the third notch and wind across the frame for two turns, and so on until the stringing of the first side has been completed. Move the string across the corner and catch it in the first notch on the adjoining side. Carry it across to the matching notch on the side opposite.

Continue the stringing in this manner until you have worked completely around the frame. Photo 1 shows the beginning of the third row of winding. Do not pull the cord tight while winding or the frame will be twisted out of shape. If this happens you will know the winding is too tight. The only solution is to unwind the cord from the frame and begin over. Leave the cords across the frame slightly slack so that the frame will lie perfectly flat on the table after it has been strung. When the stringing is complete, tie the end of the cord around the frame so it will not unwind.

The next step is to tie the threads together at each point where they cross each other. Thread a needle with matching or contrasting thread. Tie the end of this thread around the crossed threads of one point of the star. Bring the thread around the joint in both directions in a "cross-stitch" type of tie. Secure it by knotting on the under side of the doily (this is the side being worked on in photo 2), then bring the thread to the next crossing

10

point and secure it in both directions again. Work along the row of joints, crossing each one in all directions (there are three sets of crossing threads in the center portion) until the opposite point of the star is reached. Tie all the joints in this manner.

Remove the doily from the frame by clipping the threads at the notches, as in photo 3. This leaves an uneven fringe all around. Clip all the fringe threads to an even length of about 1″ (photo 4), to complete the doily.

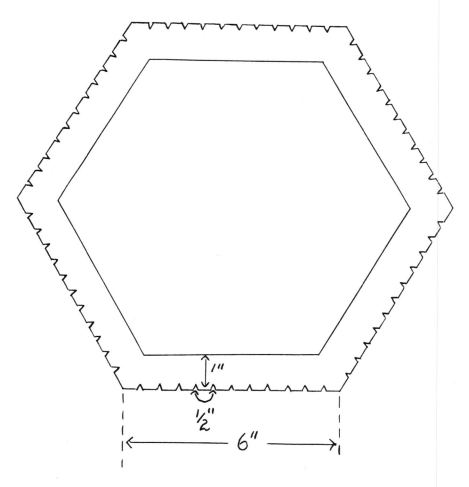

1″

½″

←——— 6″ ———→

SNOWFLAKE DOILY FRAME

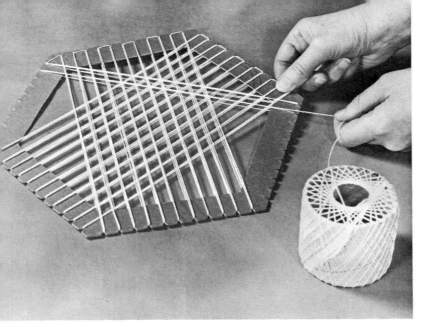

1. String the frame by wrapping the cord across from one side to the opposite side, catching the cord in the matching notches. Take two turns around the frame, then move over to the next set of notches and continue the stringing, working on around the frame.

2. Tie the threads together at each point of crossing, passing the thread around the joint in both directions of the points of the star, and in all three directions in the center portion of the doily. Use a "cross-stitch" type of tie and secure the thread on the under side by knotting before moving on to the next joint.

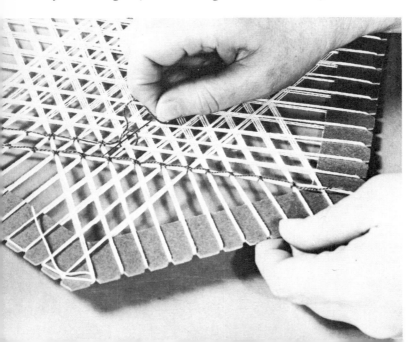

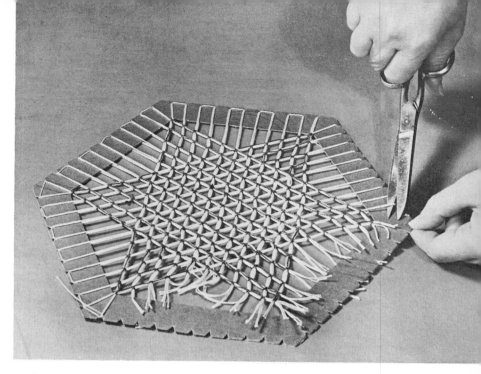

3. *After the tying of all the joints is completed, clip the threads at the notches to remove the doily from the frame.*

4. *Trim all of the fringe threads to the same length.*

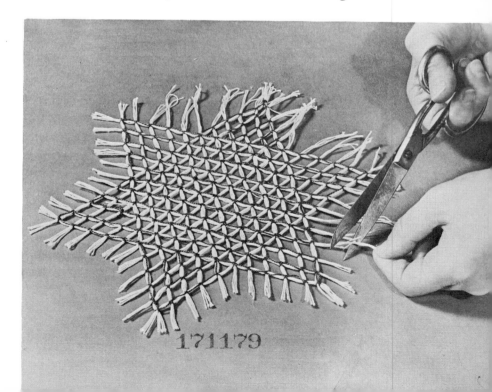

171179

Chapter 2

A CHINESE TOP

Helicopters are odd hybrids of whose principle men have dreamed since ancient times when they first wished to fly like birds, but have finally applied to practical use only in the last quarter century.

One of the first to actually fly was built in Russia in 1910. It could lift itself but not a pilot. Two years later a 'copter was built in Denmark that could carry a pilot and fly—but only about three feet off the ground. It wasn't until 1939 that the first successful flight was made. Since then improvements have been made rapidly and many uses have been found for the Jack-of-all-trades conveyances that have been called "Flying Windmills," "Eggbeaters," or "Whirlybirds." They have given ranchers a lift to check on widely-scattered herds, and carried trouble shooters on inspection tours of isolated power lines. They have been used in exploring for oil, for dusting crops and for fighting forest fires. Rescue work can be accomplished by helicopter when it is impossble to reach the victim in any other way.

The Chinese have been credited with making the very first helicopter centuries ago. It could not carry passengers and didn't look like present day ones but the idea was there in the toy which has since come to be called a Chinese Top. It was simply a vertical shaft with a propeller fastened to its top. When twirled between the palms and released, shaft and propeller whirled off.

Here is a modern version of the ancient top, the ancestor of the "whirlybird", which has the propeller separated from the shaft. It is sent whirling up through the air by a "launcher" when a quick pull is given to the string wrapped around it.

To make one you will need an empty gallon-size plastic jug, two large-size thread spools, a piece of an old broomstick handle, a metal washer, a piece of ¼″ dowel, two small nails and some string.

Cut off the bottom of the jug. Make a paper pattern for the propeller as shown in the diagram and in photo 1. It should be the same diameter as the bottom of the jug. A jigsaw or coping saw should be used for cutting away the inner portions since the bottom is too thick to be easily cut otherwise. Drill two holes, ½″ apart, through the center section.

Light a candle and hold the propeller above it with the heat concentrated at a joint of the propeller and rim. When the plastic softens sufficiently, give the blade a slight twist to bend the left-hand edge of the blade a little above the rim and the right hand edge a little below it. Hold it in position until the plastic hardens. This will take only a few minutes. Twist the other three blades in the same manner. (photo 2)

Saw one of the thread spools in half. Set it on top of the other spool. Cut a piece of ¼″ diameter dowel ½″ longer than the combined height of the spool and a half. Saw 6″ off the broomstick to make the handle of the launcher. Drill a ¼″ diameter hole into the cut end of the stick to a depth of ½″. Force one end of the dowel into the hole (see photo 3). Slip the half-spool onto the dowel, flange end up, and glue it to the top of the handle (photo 4). Drive two small nails into one end of the other spool, as far apart as the holes in the propeller center. Clip off the nails as in photo 5, about ¼″ above the spool. File the ends to smooth, rounded points.

You are now ready to send your propeller spinning. Slip a washer onto the dowel against the half-spool. Set the holes in the center of the propeller over the nail pegs in the spool, (photo 7). Give the string wrapped around the spool a strong, steady pull and your Chinese Top will be airborne.

15

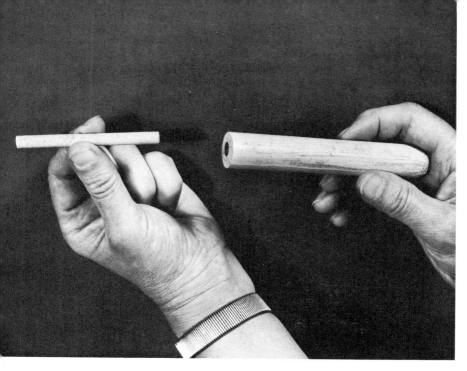

3. Force the length of 1/4" dowel into the hole in the broomstick handle.

4. Slip the half-spool down onto the dowel. Glue the spool to the top of the handle.

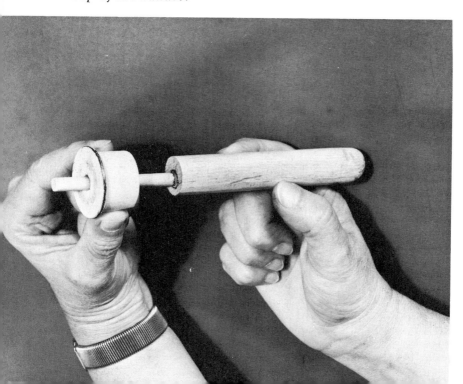

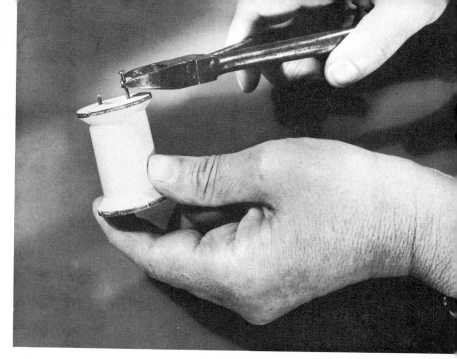

5. Drive nails into the top of the spool. Clip off the heads leaving about 1/4" protruding. File the clipped ends to smooth, rounded points.

6. Place a washer on top of the half-spool and slide the spool with the prongs onto the dowel. It should spin easily.

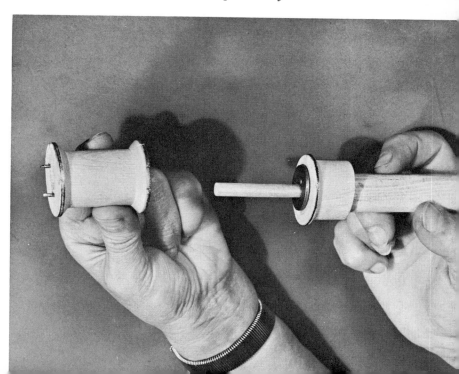

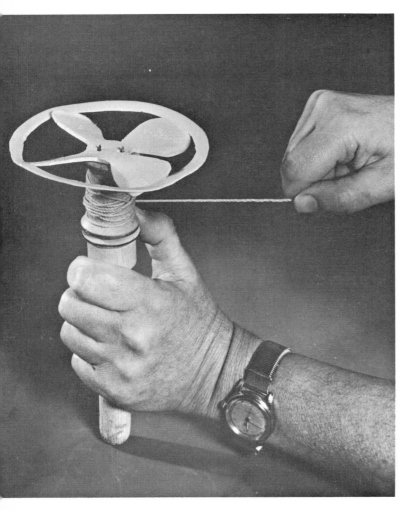

7. *Wind the string around the spool. Fit the propeller onto the prongs and give the string a quick, steady pull to spin the propeller into the air.*

Chapter 3

CORSAGE PIN-PURSE

Italy always has been, and still is, famous for the fine leathercraft articles that are produced there. Way back in the 11th century a lady of the nobility, Mathilde of Tuscany, wanted something different than all the other ladies were wearing. She designed a little leather purse that she could hang onto the loop of her jeweled cloth belt. The purse was to be placed on one hip so that it would look like an ornament, yet it would give her a fine place to carry her valuables. She went to the man who usually made her fine leather sandals and explained her idea to him. He had never seen anything of the sort but he had a good imagination and was a fine craftsman. Before long the lady wore her hip purse and was the envy of all her friends. But not for long. Others used the idea and soon the little purses were "high fashion" not only in Florence, Italy, where the first one was made, but all over Europe as well. They were made in many different shapes and dressed up with gold, precious stones, embroidery, ribbons, tassels and even flowers, making them very fancy ornaments indeed, which quite hid their real purpose, a handy way to carry money wherever the lady went.

Borrowing the idea of that Italian lady, why not make a corsage purse that looks like a bouquet of flowers to be worn on your shoulder, or pinned to your sash type belt. The little purse, completely hidden by the flowers, is a fine place to carry small change. Then you will always have nickels, dimes and pennies for the parking meter or for making a phone call. This is not intended to replace your billfold but as a handy place to carry emergency money.

21

The purse and the flowers that decorate it are made of felt. If you prefer, you can use art foam for the flowers. Or you might even make the entire piece, purse and flowers, from scraps of soft leather cut from old purses or gloves. Whatever the material, the technique of making it is exactly the same.

Cut out the purse, using the pattern given. Blanket stitch around the opening edge, A. Then fold up the front portion, B, against the back, C, and blanket stitch around the entire purse as shown in photo 1.

Sew the two parts of a snap to the inside of the flap and to the front of the purse for a closure. Sew a pin to the back. This may be either an ordinary safety pin or one of the pin backs, with holes for sewing, that are used for jewelry making.

Two kinds of flowers were used for our corsage, roses and a daisy type. Cut seven petals for each rose using the pattern given. Roll one petal tightly to form the center of the flower. Stitch it at the bottom to keep it from unrolling. Arrange the rest of the petals around the center, stitching each one to the bottom of the center as the flower is formed. Photo 2 shows the center with two petals stitched to it, the other four petals still to be put on, and a completed rose.

For the "daisy" cut a strip of eight or nine petals using the pattern given. Continue the strip beyond the dotted line of the pattern until the desired number of petals are cut. Gather the bottom of the strip with needle and thread and arrange the petals into a single or a double flower. Photo 3 shows the gathering and one arrangement of the petals. Matching thread should be used instead of the light colored thread being used in the photo for purposes of clarity. Sew a circle of yellow felt to the center to hide the gathered petal ends.

Stitch the daisy to the flap of the purse near the bottom edge, as shown in photo 4. Arrange roses, buds and leaves around the daisy to make an attractive corsage and completely hide the purse. When you are satisfied with the arrangement, stitch each flower and leaf in place to the flap and to the front of the purse to finish the corsage pin-purse as shown in photo 5.

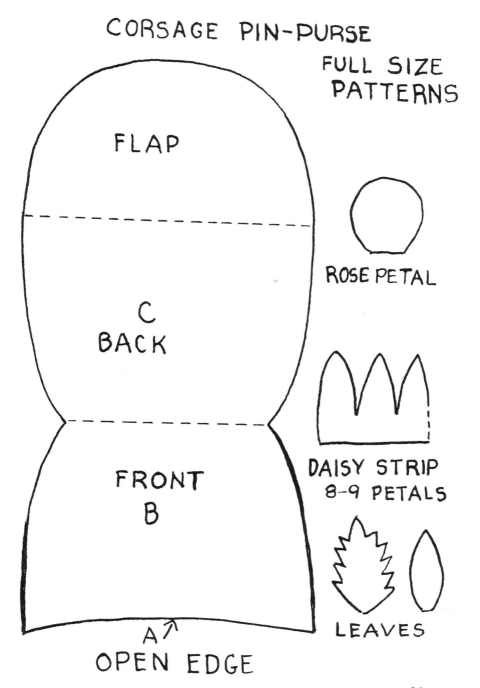

CORSAGE PIN-PURSE

FULL SIZE
PATTERNS

FLAP

C
BACK

ROSE PETAL

DAISY STRIP
8-9 PETALS

FRONT
B

LEAVES

A
OPEN EDGE

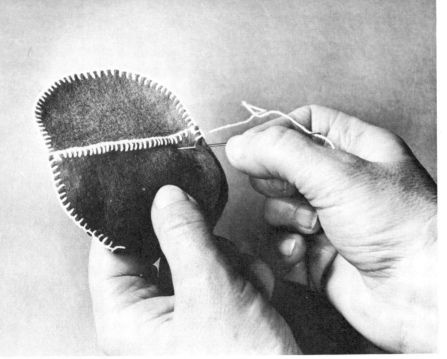

1. *Blanket stitch all around the purse to fasten the edges together.*

2. *Roll up one petal tightly to form the rose center. Stitch it at the bottom to keep it from unrolling. Arrange the rest of the petals around the center, stitching each petal to it before adding the next.*

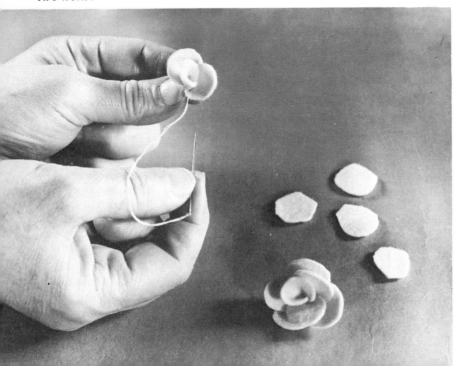

3.   Gather the strip of daisy petals along the bottom and arrange the petals to form a single or double flower. Stitch on a yellow center to hide the gathered edge.

4.   Stitch the daisy to the flap, near the bottom edge.

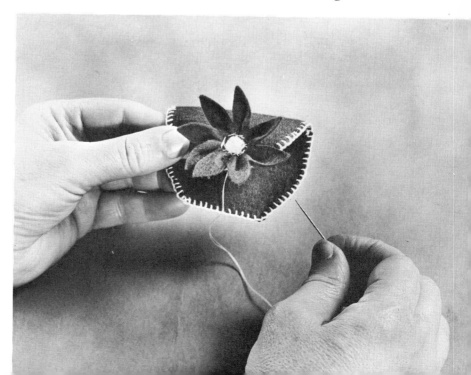

5. *It looks like a corsage and it is, but it is also a purse for small change hidden by the flowers and leaves.*

Chapter 4

INDIAN BASKETS

At about the time that Christ was born, wandering Indians came from the north to what we now call the "Four Corners" area where the edges of the states of Colorado, Utah, Arizona and New Mexico come together. They were a farming people who established homes on top of the mesas high above the surrounding plains. Here they lived and farmed for 1300 years. Then, for reasons that archeologists can only guess at, they left the mesa tops never to return. Later, Spanish explorers named the place Mesa Verde, or "green table."

When the Indians first came to the area they did not know how to make pottery but used baskets instead. For about 450 years, baskets were their only containers and consequently the Indians who live on the mesa during that time have been named Basket Makers. As the name suggests, basket making was the major craft and they were used for all household purposes where containers were needed. They were cleverly woven and artistically decorated and of a variety of different shapes. Shallow trays were common but there were also bowls, deep carrying baskets, in which they probably carried home their field crops of corn and squash, and quite small ones that are believed to have been used for "jewel boxes" or for storing ceremonial objects. Some were so tightly woven that they could be used for carrying and storing water and even for cooking. The cooking baskets were not placed directly on the fire, however. Instead, the food was placed into the basket and covered with water. Stones were heated in the fire until they were very hot, then they were dropped into the basket to heat the water and cook the food. When they cooled, they were fished out and fresh hot stones were dropped in. Cooking dinner by this method was a slow process and quite likely the cook's fingers were burned long before the stew was ready, so the Indians generally ate half-cooked food.

The fibers of yucca, a spiny, spike-leafed plant that grows in the Southwest, were used for making the baskets. They were either coiled or plated. Pueblo Indians of the Southwest, who are the descendents of those early Basket Makers, still use much the same method for making baskets today.

A COILED BASKET

Instead of using yucca, you can make a coiled basket using braided cotton clothesline rope for the core of the coil, and strips of stretched and twisted crepe paper for the wrapping. Though your materials are different, the technique is the same as that used by the Indians. One hank of clothesline rope will make several baskets.

The basket shown is in two colors. Prepare a strip of crepe paper in each color before you begin forming the basket. Cut through the entire thickness of the fold of paper, across the grain. Make the strips about ½″ wide. Stretch and slightly twist the entire length of each strip. It is easier to work with fairly short pieces of paper so cut off about a 2 foot long piece to begin with. Glue the paper around one end of the clothesline rope. Thread the other end of the strip into the eye of a darning needle. Wrap the paper around the rope in overlapping spirals so that the rope is completely covered. After you have wrapped for about 1½″, roll the covered rope into a tight, flat coil and bind it to itself, using the knot stitch, as follows:

Pass the wrapping around the coil being worked on and the coil against which it lies, from back to front. Carry the wrapping over the front of the two coils, across the top and to the back again. Bring the needle to the front passing it between the two coils on the right of the wrapping (Fig. 1). Pass the needle across the wrapping and between the two coils to the back, on the left, as in Fig. 2. Draw the stitch tight. Cross over the wrapping of the two coils on the back side and bring the needle to the front again, between the coils, on the right side of the wrapping. see Fig. 3. Draw the strip snug to complete the knot. Continue the wrapping around the rope, as in Fig. 4, for four or five turns, then bind the coils together with another knot stitch. Continue forming the flat bottom of the basket in this way. Put on the same number of wrapping turns between each knot stitch. Photo 1 shows the first few completed coils of the basket bottom, with a knot just finished and ready to continue the wrapping of the rope. Add to the wrapping strip as needed by gluing on additional pieces of the stretched crepe paper.

The basket may be made in a single color or you may wish to work out a design in two colors as in the one illustrated. When working in more than one color, thread a needle with a strip of each. Hold the strip of the second color of paper along the inside of the rope and carry the wrapping over both the rope and the paper. When the second color is used to make the design, carry the strip of the first color along the rope and wrap with the second color for the desired length, as shown in photo 2. A design should always begin in line with the place where the second coil is begun at the center of the basket bottom, and then be evenly spaced around the basket. The beginning stitch of the darker color can be identified in photo 3.

After the flat bottom of the basket is as large as desired, begin to shape the sides by setting the coils above each other instead of continuing in a flat spiral. If they are set directly one on top of the other, you will have a straight sided basket. To make a bowl shape similar to the one shown, set each coil on a slight slant just a bit above and outside the previous one as in photo 3. You will quickly learn how to place the coils to produce whatever shape you wish.

To add handles, wrap the rope for about 4″ without knotting it to the previous coil. Bring the end of the wrapped portion down against the coil, with the center curving away from the basket, and knot it to the coil. Continue wrapping and knotting until you have worked around the basket to a point opposite the first handle. Form the second handle in the same manner, see photo 4. Proceed with the wrapping and knotting until you are within 1″ of the first handle. Cut off the rope so that the end will just reach to the beginning of the handle. Taper the end of the rope so that it ends against the previous coil without a noticeable bump. Finish wrapping and knotting to the end of the rope at the point where the handle begins. Glue down the end of the paper strip. Give the basket two coats of clear shellac to stiffen it and produce a shiny finish that will be easy to wipe clean. The completed basket is shown in photo 5.

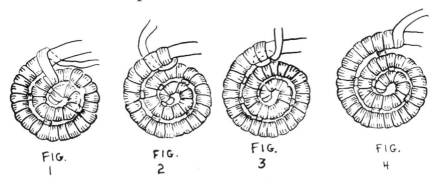

FIG.
1

FIG.
2

FIG.
3

FIG.
4

1. Wrap the rope for about 1 1/2". Roll it into a tight coil and knot the beginning of the second coil to the end of the first. Wrap the rope for about five turns of the crepe paper strip, knot again. Continue the wrapping and knotting, keeping the coils flat.

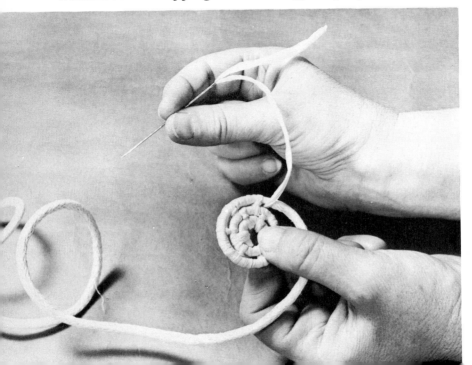

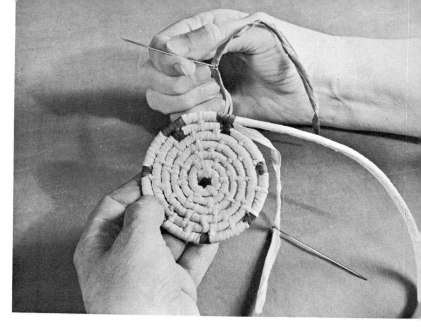

2. When working with two colors, thread each color of crepe paper into a needle. Lay one strand of the paper along the rope and wrap over rope and paper with the other color for as far as need be. Then reverse the strips of crepe paper and wrap with the second color while the first is carried along the rope.

3. Form a flat coil for the base, then begin building up the basket shape by raising each coil slightly on the one before it, to form a bowl shape.

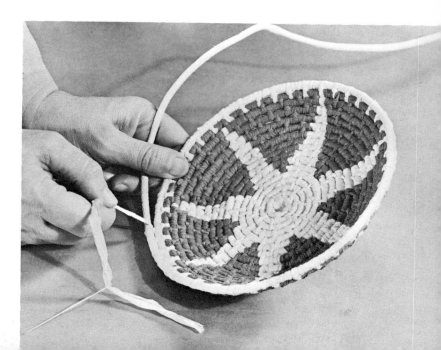

4.   Handles may be formed during the wrapping of the last row. Wrap without knotting, a length of about 4". Curve the wrapped portion back against the row before it and knot, then continue wrapping and knotting until the point on the rim just opposite the first handle is reached. Form the second handle, then continue the wrapping and knotting to finish the top of the basket at the place where the first handle was formed.

5.   Give the completed basket two coats of shellac to stiffen it and provide an easy-clean finish.

Chapter 5

EGYPTIAN JEWELRY

In ancient Egypt, jewelry was an important part of every person's costume. Precious stones and gold were much used. Old pictures show that men, as well as women even used necklaces. Some handsome jewelry pieces have been discovered in old Egyptian tombs as a person's belongings were often buried with him so that he could use them in the next world. Some of these may now be seen in museums. Gold wire was often rolled into flat coils and assembled to make arm bands, pins, rings and neck bands. This type of jewelry is still called Egyptian jewelry today. It is handsome, but easy to make and quite inexpensive if you use 16 gauge copper wire. Sterling silver wire is also available and may be used but it is more expensive.

The basic unit of Egyptian jewelry is the flat, coiled, double spiral made from a single piece of wire. The coiling is done from each end with a length of straight wire left between the two units. This wire is bent into a loop hook for linking into the next unit. Units are linked together until the joined pieces are as long as necessary. Pins and pendants may also be made of coiled units without the center hooks.

Following are directions for making a bracelet, a necklace pendant and a pin.

BRACELET. Cut pieces of wire 6″ long. If wire thinner than 16 gauge is used longer pieces will be needed. Mark the center of each piece of wire with a crayon. Use a long-nosed pair of pliers to bend each end of the wire into as small a loop as possible. Pinch the loops tight. Hold one of the loops flat in the tip of the pliers and bend the wire around against itself to form a coil. Bend only a short distance before moving the coil be tight against the one before it and the coil will remain flat as in photo 1. Coil the wire until you are within ¾″ of the center mark. Form the coil from the other end of the wire in the same manner. There should be 1½″ length of wire left between the two coils. Bend this into a loop with the edges of the coils touching each other. Make 16 more units in the same manner. Be sure that the coils are the same size so that the units will be as identical as possible. Cut a piece of wire 8″ long and form one more unit. Roll the coils the same size as those of the other units, leaving the loop wire longer. This will be used for the hook unit of the bracelet.

Lay the coils on a firm wood surface and pound each with a mallet to flatten the wire.

Bend the loop of one of the coils down and back against itself so that the loop extends beyond the bottoms of the coils on the back side. Bend the loop of a second coil unit until it is at a right angle to the coils. Slip this loop through the loop of unit No. 1. Continue bending the loop of unit No. 2 until it is back against itself with the end beyond the bottoms of the coils. Photo 2 shows how the units are linked together.

Continue linking until all of the units have been joined, using the unit with the long loop last. Bend the end of this loop into a hook. Use a piece of wire 1″ long to form a ring for the other end of the bracelet. Leave the ends apart just enough to slip them into the bend between the loop and the coils of the first section as in photo 3. Use the pliers to pinch the ends of the wire together. The ring extends beyond the coils so that the hook may be slipped into it to fasten the bracelet around the wrist.

A necklace may be made in exactly the same manner using as many linked coils as are necessary to make it the desired length.

forward in the jaws of the pliers so that each circle of wire will

PENDANT. Cut a piece of wire 15" long. Double it at the center and pinch the bend tight with the pliers. Form the double wire into a loop, then coil just as you did the single wires for the bracelet units. Bend the inner wire for a length of about 1", then work the outer wire against it for the same distance, then the inner wire again, and so on until about 4" is left of each end of the wire, see photo 4. Make a loop at the free end of one of the pieces and coil it until it is against the larger coil. Do the same with the other free end of the wire (photo 5). Cut a piece of wire 2½" long. Bend the wire into a loop at the center with the ends crossing each other. Flatten the coiled pendant and the loop wire. Bend the ends of the legs and slip them through the center loops of the two smaller spirals. Pinch the ends of the wires tight against the backs of the spirals. Grasp the loop in the jaws of the pliers and give it a half twist so that when it is slipped onto the necklace chain the coils will lie flat.

BAR PIN. For this four-spiral lap pin, cut two pieces of wire each 9" long. Bend the beginning loop at one end of a wire and coil it to the center. At the other end of the wire, bend the starting loop in the opposite direction and coil this half of the wire to the center also. Coil the second piece of wire into an identical double reverse spiral. Flatten both sets of spirals. Push one of the spirals of a pair behind the other for about half its width so that one laps over the other. Photo 6 shows one of the double spirals after it has been coiled and flattened but before lapping, and the other spiral from the back side as it is bent to lap. Bend the second unit in the same manner. Cement the two units together, lapping them so that the bar appears to be four individual spirals. Use epoxy cement to join the two units and to attach a pin back.

Give the jewelry a coat of fingernail polish or laquer to keep it bright and shining.

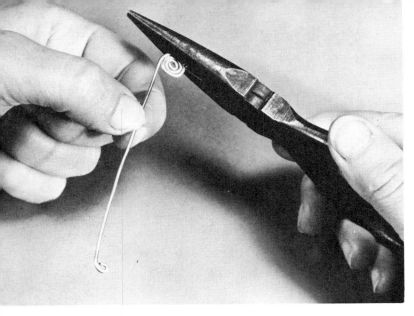

1. Bend as small a loop as possible into each end of the wire. Hold the loop flat in the jaws of the pliers and bend the wire into a tight, flat coil.

2. Bend the wire between the coils into a loop. Bend the loop down, then back against itself so that it extends beyond the bottom of the coils. Bend the loop of the second unit at a right angle. Slip it through the loop of the first unit to join the two, then continue bending it back against itself until the loop extends beyond the coils. Continue hooking together the units until you have sufficient length for the bracelet.

3. Bend the loop of the last unit, which is longer than the others, into a hook. Attach a loop of wire to the other end so that the bracelet may be clasped.

4. For the pendant, bend the wire double at the center and roll a double coil until the ends of the wire beyond it are 4″ long.

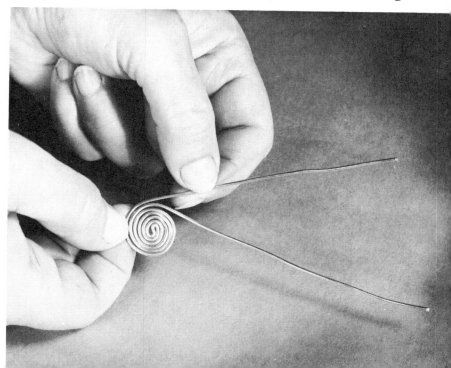

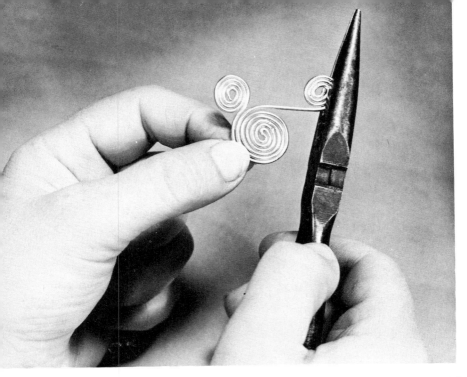

5. Bend the free ends of the wire into two smaller, individual coils.

6. Make two units of lapped, spiral coils for the bar pin. Lap and cement the units together with epoxy cement.

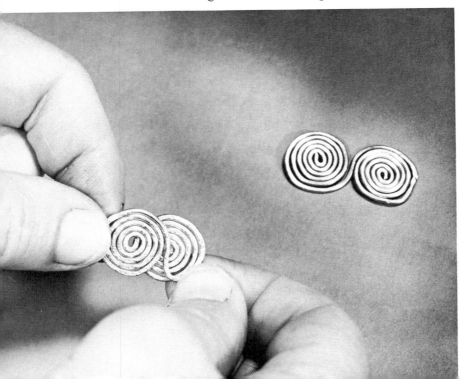

7.   The bar pin, the necklace pendant and the bracelet are three examples of coiled wire Egyptian Jewelry.

Chapter 6

HORN BUGLE

Do you play some kind of a "horn" in the school band? Have you ever wondered why some instruments are called horns? Probably not, because certain wind instruments have had that name for so long we never think of them by any other. They were originally given that name because the "ancestors" of the cone-shaped instruments that have no side holes were made of ram horn or cattle horn.

Who blew the first one?

The bugle and the trumpet are instruments of great antiquity. One of this type, the shofar, made of ram's horn was the "trumpet" used by the Hebrews at Jericho according to the account in Joshua 6: 4, 5. Gideon, too, used a massed band of 300 of the shofar, to terrorize the Midianites, as told in Judges 7.

More recently in Europe, where hunting was a popular sport, the "Hunter's Horn" was an important part of the equipment, and the first ones were made of true horn. Symbolic ones were even used as a badge of knighthood by one group organized in the 15th century. Knights who were members of "The Order of the Horn" wore collars of golden hunting horns.

You can make a horn much like those ancient instruments, from a natural cow's horn. It is played in the same way as a bugle or trumpet and makes a fine dinner horn to use at camp, or just an instrument to have fun with. With a little practice you will be able to play it.

You can get a horn from a slaughtering house. The size will make a difference in the tone. A small one will be shrill and can be heard for a great distance. A larger horn will have a more mellow sound but not as great carrying power.

If it is not cleaned out, boil the horn until the inside can be removed. The horn itself will be softened when you remove it from the water. Scrape the outside to remove any scaliness. It will harden quite quickly again so you must work fast, or return it to the water to soften again.

Clamp the horn tip in a vise and use a hacksaw to cut off the horn about 3″ from the tip, as in photo 1. The short piece will be the mouthpiece. Saw off the extreme tip where it measures about ⅝″ diameter.

Bore a ⅜″ diameter hole through the mouthpiece at the narrow end. Use a file to enlarge the opening of the mouthpiece at the larger end, photo 2. The wall should be no more than ⅛″ thick.

Enlarge the hole at the cut end of the horn with the round file until this wall, too, is about ⅛″ thick (photo 3).

Fit the narrow end of the mouthpiece into the opening in the end of the horn. If necessary, dress the mouthpiece down to fit tightly into the opening, photo 4. After it fits properly, remove the mouthpiece again.

Use a rasp to finish removing any roughness from the outside of the horn. Then scrape it with a piece of glass to thin down the wall and improve the resonance (photo 5). Scraping is easier if you boil the horn again and scrape while it is soft. Finish the smoothing job with fine emery cloth, then steel wool. Wax and polish the pieces to a high gloss.

File a groove around the horn 1″ back from the large end, and another ½″ from the cut end (photo 6). Use a leather boot lace for a carrying thong. Tie the ends around the horn in the grooves. Glue in the mouthpiece. Photo 7 shows the completed horn.

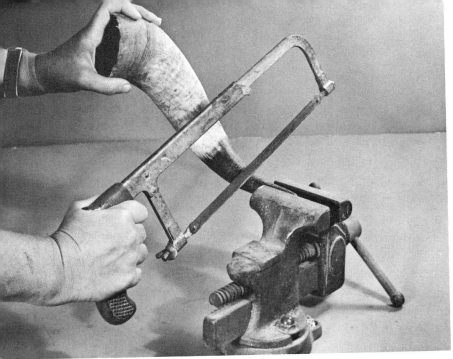

1.   Saw off about 3" of the tip end of the horn for a mouthpiece.
Then saw off the extreme tip where the horn is about 5/8" diameter.

2.   Bore a 3/8" diameter hole through the tip of the mouthpiece.
Then use a round file to enlarge the hole into the mouthpiece at
the large end. The wall should be no more than 1/8" thick.

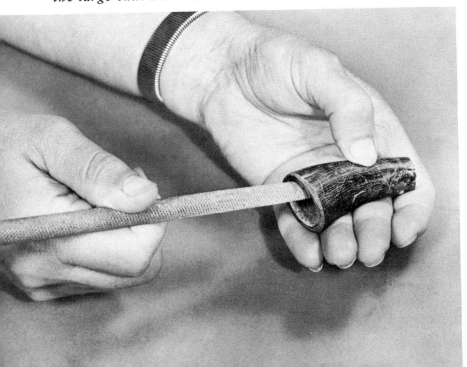

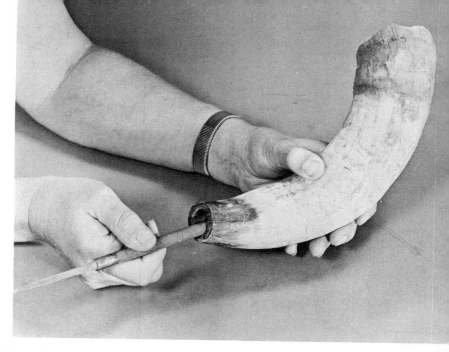

3. Use the round file to enlarge the hole at the end of the horn. This wall, too, should be no more than 1/8" thick.

4. Twist the narrow end of the mouthpiece into the end of the horn, checking for fit. You may have to enlarge the opening in the end of the horn or dress down the mouthpiece to get a good tight fit. Remove the mouthpiece again.

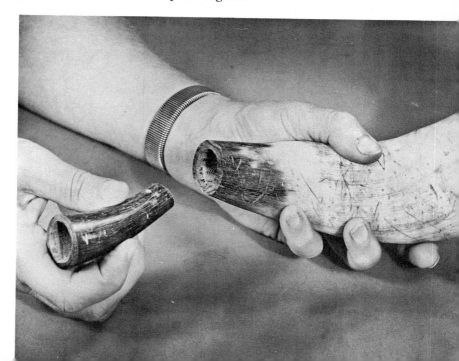

5. Finish the smoothing of the outside of the horn and mouth-piece. Use a rasp to remove the rough parts. Boiling the horn will soften it enough to make scraping it with a piece of glass or a knife blade easier. Finish by rubbing with fine emery cloth, then steel wool until it is smooth. Wax it and polish to a bright shine.

6. Use a three-cornered file to cut a groove around the horn about 1" back from the large end and about 1/2" from the cut end.

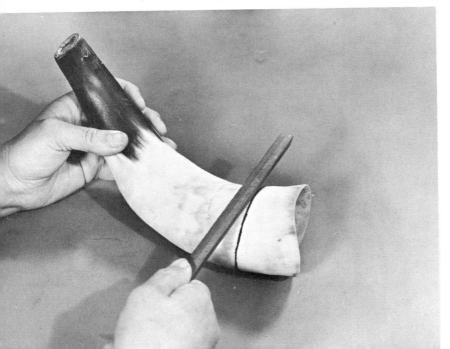

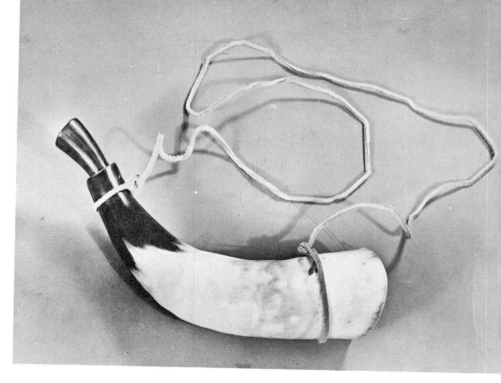

7. *A rawhide boot lace makes a good leather thong to tie around the bugle in the two grooves. Glue the mouthpiece in place and the bugle is finished.*

Chapter 7

THE DREIDEL OF ISRAEL

A favorite toy of the children of Israel is the Dreidel. It is used for a special game during the week of celebration of the Jewish "Feast of Lights." Jewish children in America like to play with it also.

The Dreidel (the Hebrew name is "Sevivon" and both names mean "going around") is a four-sided top, rather tall for its width. On each side is a Hebrew letter, initials for the four words of the phrase "Nes gadol hayah sham," which translated means a "great miracle happened there." The first letter of the first word is "nun" or "n"; the first letter of the second word is "gimel" or "g"; the first letter of the third word is "hay" or "h"; and the first letter of the fourth word is "shin" or "sh."

Directions for playing the game come from the German interpretations of the dreidel letters. The "n" stands for "nichts" or *nothing;* the "g" stands for "ganz" or *all;* "h" stands for "halb" or *half;* and the "sh" for "stell" or *put.* Nuts, candies or raisins can be used and any number can play (instead of the traditional holiday goodies the game could be played with beans or marbles for counters). The children decide, before play begins, how much each will put into the "kitty" at the start of each game. Each takes a turn at spinning the dreidel. Whatever letter is on the upper face when the top falls indicates what the player must do. If it is a "gimel" he may take all of the jackpot; if it is "hay" he may take half; "nun" means he gets nothing at all; and for "shin" he must put into the kitty whatever was decided at the beginning of the game.

Dreidels come in all colors, sizes and materials, but the shape is always the same with four flat sides. Our Dreidel is made of a 1½″ square piece of wood, 2½″ long. You can make it larger or smaller as you wish. Round off one end to make the blunt point. This may be done by carving with a knife, or on a turning lathe. Drill a hole, ½″ deep and ¼″ in diameter, into the center of the end opposite the point. Glue a piece of ¼″ dowel into the hole to make the spinning handle. Paint one of the letters on each side of the dreidel.

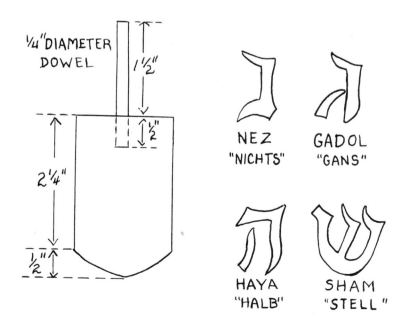

¼″ DIAMETER DOWEL

1½″

½″

2¼″

½″

NEZ
"NICHTS"

GADOL
"GANS"

HAYA
"HALB"

SHAM
"STELL"

DREIDEL

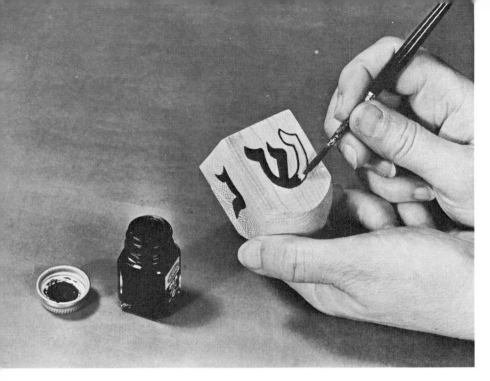

1. *Paint one of the characters on each flat face of the dreidel.*

2. *Glue the dowel handle into the hole in the center of the dreidel top.*

3. *Players take turns spinning the dreidel. It will not spin very long. The figure on the face that is uppermost when it falls determines whether the player will get all, half, or none of the goodies in the kitty, or whether he will have to add some to it from his store.*

Chapter 8

A DOOR MEZUZAH
AND PENDANTS

The people of Israel use Hebrew letters to decorate a great many objects. Jewish homes there (and most in America, too) hang a doorpiece at the entrance to the home. Though it may vary in size, shape or material of which it is made, it always has on it the Jewish letter which stands for the word "Shaddai" or "God" and is a constant reminder of the Jewish prayer which is recited as a part of every Jewish service and a symbol that God dwells in this house. The prayer is:

"Thou shalt love the Lord thy God with all thy heart, with all thy soul, and with all thy might and these words which I command thee this day, shall be upon thy heart. Thou shalt teach them diligently unto thy children and shalt speak of them when thou sittest in thy house, when thou walkest by the way, when thou liest down and when thou risest up. Thou shalt bind them for a sign upon thy hand, and they shall be for frontlets between thine eyes. Thou shalt write them upon the doorposts of thy house and upon thy gates. That ye may remember and do all my commandments and be holy unto your God."

It is said that a Jewish Rabbi once moved away and forgot to take the Mezuzah with him but left it hanging on the doorpost. The Protestant minister who moved into the house wrote to the Rabbi for an explanation of the significance and when he learned what it was, decided that the Mezuzah was so meaningful for Christians as well as Jews that he decided to leave it in place.

The Mezuzah shown here is in the shape of a pitcher, one which is often used. It is of dark wood with the letter of light

50

wood glued to it. Enlarge the pattern using 1″ squares, and make paper outline patterns for both the pitcher and the letter. Cut out the pitcher of dark wood that is ½″ thick and the letter of light wood ¼″ thick. Drill the two holes through the pitcher for attaching it to the door with screws. Carve off the edges of the pitcher and handle, then sandpaper them very smooth to give the piece a natural, rounded form, as shown in photo 1.

Glue the letter to the front of the pitcher with household cement or other waterproof glue.

Finish the Mezuzah with several coats of outdoor varnish.

People of Israel also use letters to decorate items for their own personal use. Pendants are used as necklaces or on key chains. Two shapes are shown here. Both pendants shown are decorated with the interlocking "Star of David" design plus letters. The phrase on the pendant shown used as a necklace means "luck." The letter on the key chain pendant means "life" and is often used as a good luck wish as if the giver were saying "Long life to you."

Cut the pendants from dark wood that is ⅛″ to ¼″ thick. You can use either solid wood or plywood with a walnut face. Sand them smooth. Shape the two triangles, which will be interlocked to form the star, from No. 20 copper wire. Prepare a pattern and form the triangles by laying the wire directly onto the pattern, bending the wire to fit, as in photo 1. Interlock the triangles to form the star. Lay the wire star on a piece of wood and flatten it by tapping the wire with a hammer—see photo 2. Form and flatten the letters in the same way. Use household cement to fasten the star and the letters to the wood pendant. When the cement is dry, give the entire piece, wood and wire decoration, two coats of clear fingernail polish. This gives the pendant a glossy finish and protects the wire so it will stay shiny and not tarnish.

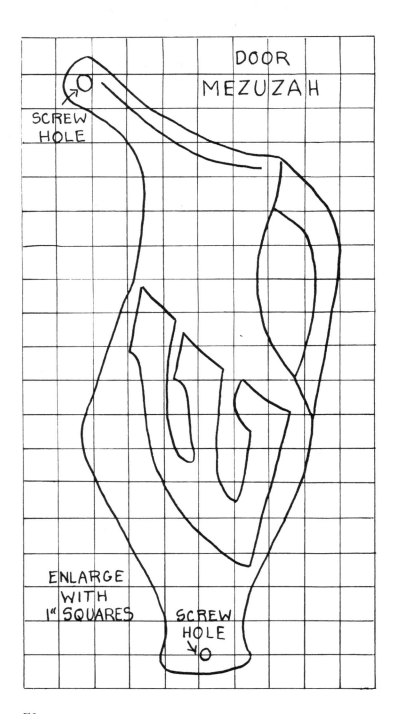

DOOR
MEZUZAH

SCREW HOLE

ENLARGE
WITH
1" SQUARES

SCREW HOLE

52

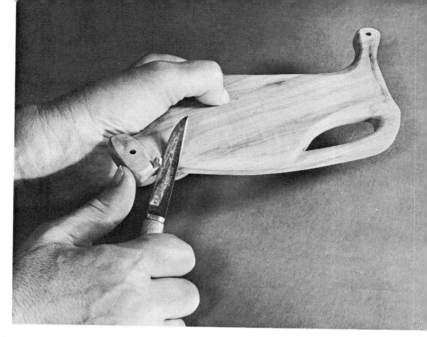

1. Cut the Mezuzah from dark hardwood (*if you wish, you may use pine and give it a coat of walnut or mahogany stain*). Round the edges with a knife and sandpaper to give a natural shape to the pitcher and handle.

2. Cut the letter from light wood. Fasten it to the Mezuzah with waterproof glue. Use an outdoor finish to weatherproof the Mezuzah. Fasten it to the door frame with screws passed through the two holes and driven into the frame.

FULL SIZE PATTERNS

WIRE TRIANGLES, FULL SIZE PATTERNS

LETTERS FULL SIZE

PHRASE SYMBOLIZES "LUCK"

LETTER "CHAIY" SIGNIFIES "LIFE"

NECKLACE OR KEY CHAIN PENDANTS

54

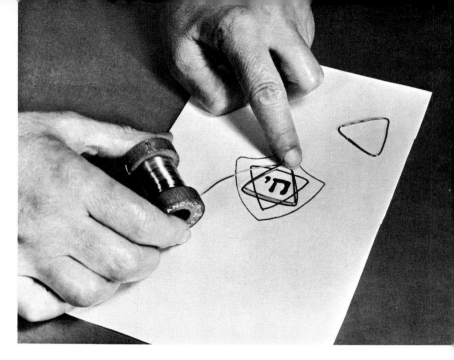

1.   *Draw the pattern for the interlocking triangles which form the star. Shape the two triangles by bending the copper wire so it lies directly on top of the paper pattern.*

2.   *Interlock the two triangles to form the star. Lay it on a piece of wood and flatten the wire by tapping with a hammer. Form the letters in the same manner.*

3. Use household cement to fasten the star and the letters to the wood pendant. Finish the piece with two coats of clear fingernail polish. The pendants can be used as necklaces or key chains.

Chapter 9

IKEBANA

The Japanese call it "Ikebana." The word means "flower arranging" but it includes, in addition to the flowers, any other materials that might be used. These could be dried materials, seed pods, leaves and branches, evergreen, vines, berries and fruits, wooden shapes or stones.

There is always an arrangement of some kind in every Japanese home. It may be only a single flower, or several graceful twigs, or it may be a very large and ornate bouquet. The housewife shops for flowers when she shops for food, every day.

On entering a room, a polite guest will always compliment the hostess on her ability and the beauty of the arrangement in its special alcove.

There are thousands of teachers of the art and hundreds of schools of flower arrangement scattered about the islands. Not only women, but many men as well, are very skillful at it.

There are a number of different types.

TSURIBANA. These are suspended flowers, usually in a basket.

KAKEBANA. These are hanging flowers too. They may be placed in baskets, pieces of bamboo stem, or ceramic bowls, as containers which are fastened to the wall.

NAGEIRA. This word originally meant "thrown-in flowers." These are in tall vases and the arrangements are less formal.

MORIBANA. These are "low-bowl" arrangements and are of five different styles; "heavenly," "cascade," "upright," "slanting," and "contrasting." Each is based on the scalene triangle— a triangle with uneven sides.

MORIMONO. This combines fruits, flowers, branches and stones in flat baskets, bowls or plates.

Containers used, besides baskets, are made of copper, bronze, or pottery, of simple design. The containers are often placed on stands or bases of some sort. These serve the double purpose of adding to the attractiveness of the arrangement and at the same time protecting the table top. Usually a square base is used with a round container, and a round base with a square container.

Slabs of polished wood are often used as bases for arrangements without containers of any sort, especially when fresh flowers are not included.

ORIENTAL PLANTER FOR PLASTIC FLOWER ARRANGEMENTS

Plastic flowers are so real looking these days, and so inexpensive and easily obtained that they are ideal for flower arrangements when you can not go out and cut a bouquet from your garden. Since they need no water, a large variety of containers can be used. This oriental type is well suited to graceful arrangements. The holes in the base make it easy to change them at your pleasure.

The main part of the planter is a square or oblong deep picture frame. The one used was about 8″ square, made of shiny black plastic. You may not find one exactly like it but can no doubt buy one that will look equally well and can be turned into a planter in the same way.

Remove the picture from the frame. This one had no glass, but if there is glass, it will not be used. Cut a piece of ¾″ thick wood, the same size as the picture. Drill a number of small holes through the wood block into which the flower stems will be fitted later. The holes should be a snug fit for the stems of the flowers you plan to use so they will not "wobble."

Make a paper pattern for each piece of the base, using ½″ squares. The two pieces are exactly the same except that the slot at the center of one is in the upper half, and in the lower half of the other. Make the slots ¼″ wide to allow the two pieces of the stand to slip together.

Cut the two pieces from ¼″ thick wood. Either plywood or solid wood may be used. If you happen to have an empty fruit crate around, wood from the side slats is fine. However, be sure to measure the thickness. If it is more or less than ¼″, make the slots the same width so the pieces fit snugly together. Sand all of the wood pieces very smooth. Slip together the two stand pieces (photo 1).

59

Turn the square piece upside down and draw a diagonal line from one corner to the opposite corner. Draw a second diagonal line connecting the other two corners. Spread glue along the top edges of the stand pieces and set them, upside down on the diagonal lines (photo 2).

After the glue has dried, make a final check of the frame on the base for fit (photo 3).

Paint the base and the stand black and when the paint has dried spread glue on the under side of the ledge on the frame and set it onto the base. The planter is now ready for you to try your hand at Ikebana.

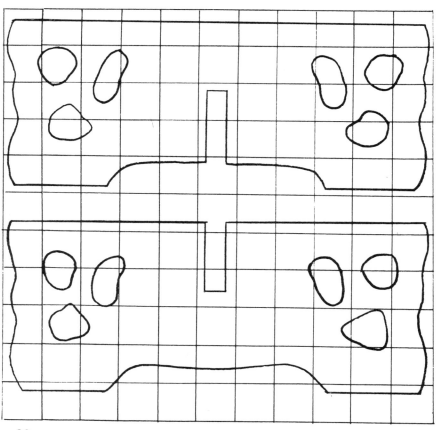

60 ENLARGE WITH ½" SQUARES

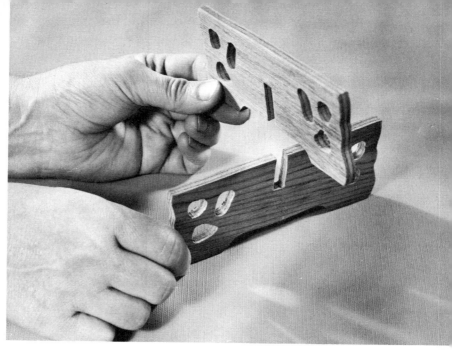

1. Slip together the two pieces of the base. A little glue in the slots will hold the two pieces tight.

2. Mark two diagonals on the under side of the base. Glue the stand in place matching the top edges to the diagonals, with the center of the stand at the crossing point of the diagonals.

3.   Make a final check for fit of the frame on the base before painting the base and stand assembly black.

4.   "Ikebana" of plastic flowers in the Oriental planter.

Chapter 10

ARRANGEMENT ON A SLAB

On your walks in Fall, keep your eyes open for seed pods, dry grasses, leaves, pine cones, acorns or any other dry material that might be combined into an arrangement. There are so many different thing that are attractive and interesting to use. Perhaps you will run across a pheasant tail feather, or a twig with dry leaves clinging to it. A stalk with several empty milkweed pods, or cat-tails are interesting materials, too. Gather up anything you see that you think you might wish to use. You will need several tall items and some short ones to make an arrangement similar to the one shown here.

Choose a base of wood. This may be a slab cut crosswise from a tree limb at least 6″ in diameter, or it may be a square or oblong piece of hardwood. Whatever you choose, the wood should be thoroughly sanded then finished with several coats of varnish or lacquer to give it a high gloss.

Set a small needlepoint holder on the wood base, near one end and to the back. Arrange the tall items in the holder, as in photo 1. These are a small cat-tail, a dry magnolia leaf and three immature seed head of sorghum with stems cut different lengths so they will be of varying heights.

Now hide the needlepoint holder and the stalks of the dry materials already in place. We began with a bronze-colored plastic dahlia, with two leaves left on the stem which was clipped to about 3″ in length. The stem was laid across the holder with the flower head resting on the base—see photo 2.

To further fill in between the flower and the upright material we tucked one seed pod from a spike of dry yucca behind the flower but in front of the stalks of the upright pieces. This hid the bases of the seed heads where they joined the stalks. A pine cone or a stubby ear of popcorn would have worked just as well as the yucca pod shown about to be tucked into place in photo 3.

Finally, finish filling in the space around the needlepoint holder to hide it completely. The prickly seed pods of sweet gum tree were used here. Acorns in their cups, or a heap of vari-colored pebbles which were thoroughly washed and dried, or any of a variety of other small items could have been used just as well. The main thing to watch here is that the pieces used are small enough that they can be fitted in the empty spaces around the bottom of the arrangement.

Your walk through the fields and woods, or along the roadside may not yield exactly the same materials as those used in the completed arrangement shown in photo 4, but you will doubtless find some that can be used to make an equally attractive one.

1. Set a small needlepoint holder on the wood base and push the stems of the taller items in place.

2. Lay a plastic flower or suitable piece of dried material such as a fungus, on the slab, beginning the hiding of the needlepoint holder.

3. *Build up the arrangement behind the flower to tie the base to the upright parts. A yucca seed pod tucked between the flower and the stems was used here.*

4. *The completed slab arrangement.*

Chapter 11

PEASANT BAG

The people of Greece consider their peasant bags one of the handiest things they can own. Everybody uses a bag to carry whatever must be taken along or brought back home, whenever he goes anywhere. Women use them for groceries. Children find them handy to carry school books and papers, and a Greek shepherd will pack his lunch of bread and cheese into a bag each morning. It is then slung over his shoulder and lunch is ready wherever he happens to be when the sun says it is noon.

The bag is made of a piece of coarse, heavy material, twice as long as it is wide. It is embroidered with bright colored yarn in a design that completely covers the background. It is considered a poor job if any of the background shows. The completed piece of embroidery is folded double, the sides are seamed together and the open top is finished. The heavy yarn braid which forms the handle is nearly four feet long. This is a convenient length when a man wears the bag over his shoulder but is too long a handle for women and children so it is simply tied into a knot to make it whatever length is most convenient. The end of the handle, where the braid is finished, is raveled out to form three little bright colored tassels.

You can make a bag similar to the ones used in Greece, using a piece of burlap or other heavy, loosely woven material for the background cloth. A piece measuring 14" x 28" will make a handy size bag.

Lay out the guide lines of the embroidery design on the background material, using a ruler and a china marking pencil, or a pencil with a soft lead, as in photo 1.

Embroider the design with 4-ply yarn in whatever bright colors you wish. Leave the stitches rather loose so they fluff together and completely cover the background—photo 2. When the embroidery is completed, fold the piece double and seam up the sides. In Greece this is done by hand with an overcast stitch in a "figure 8" so that the edge appears to be braided. If you wish, the seaming can be done on the sewing machine. Finish off the top. The Greek bag shown has a fancy edging but a simple hem is quite satisfactory.

Cotton rug yarn is good for making the braided handle. Cut nine strands each 72″ long. Lay them out, side by side, and tie a cord around the center of the strands as in photo 3. Double the strands back over the tying cord. You will now have six strands of each color of yarn. Use each group as a single strand for making the three-strand braid. Braid to within 8″ of the end. Tie a cord around the strands of one color, close against the braid. Cut off the strands 2″ beyond the tie and ravel out the free ends to make a tassel. Braid the strands of the second color together for a length of 1½″, then tie the strands into a knot to keep the braid from opening. Braid the strands of the third color together for a length of 2″. Tie the ends around the braid of the second color, just above the knot—photo 4. Cut off the strands of both colors, leaving free ends 2″ long. Unravel the ends to make tassels. The three tassels are distinguishing characteristics of the Greek bag. Sew the ends of the handle securely to the side seams.

1. Use a ruler and a china marking pencil (or an ordinary pencil with a soft lead) to lay out the embroidery design on the burlap.

2. Use 4-ply yarn in whatever bright colors you wish, to fill in the design solid so that none of the burlap shows.

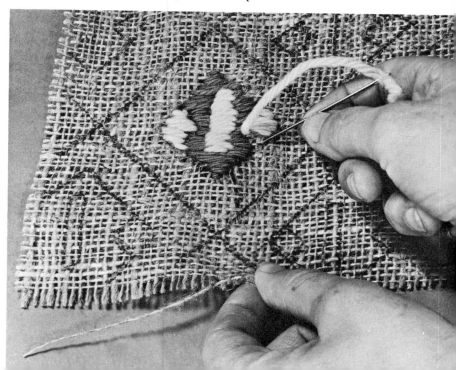

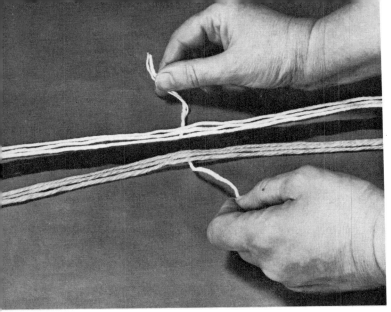

3. Lay out the nine strands of rug yarn for the braided handle. Tie them together at the center, then double the strands, making six strands of each color for making the three-strand braid.

4. Braid the strands together until you are within about 8″ of the end. Tie a cord tightly around the six strands of one color. Cut off the strands about 2″ below the tying cord and unravel the strands to make a tassel. Divide the other two colors. Make a three-strand braid of one color for a length of about 1 1/2″. Tie the strands into a knot. Braid the other color for about 2″, then separate the strands and bring them around the other braid, just above the knot. Tie the strands around the braid and fringe the ends.

5.   *This bag was made in Greece. Women use the bags for shop-*
ping, children use them for carrying schoolbooks, and shepherds
pack their lunch of bread and cheese in them and sling them over
the shoulder when they go to work in the morning.

Chapter 12

MEXICAN FIESTA STRING

In Mexico, many interesting and useful things are made from gourds. The gourds are of many different sizes and shapes, and some of them resemble certain things. One kind looks like the body of a bird with a long, curving neck, and that is just what the Mexican craftsmen make of them. They add a bill and long legs, then lacquer the birds in brilliant colors, blue, orange, red or yellow.

Each Mexican state, and often each town, specializes in some craft. Tehauantepec, a town in the south part of the country, is well known for its hicaras. They are bowls made of large gourds, which the women use instead of baskets, to carry their groceries home from market, balancing them on their heads. The hicaras are usually painted bright red inside and yellow outside. The outside is further decorated with gay bands of color, or bright wreaths of flowers. Often, at the very bottom of the bowl in the natural hollow of the gourd, a pink flower is put on for a final touch of decoration, contrasting pleasantly with the yellow background.

The large gourds grow only in the warmer parts of North America, but small gourds can be used to make attractive decorations too. They grow almost anywhere and you can get a package of mixed gourd seed from any seed catalogue and grow your own. If you have no place to plant a garden, dime stores or florist shops usually have gourds for sale in the fall. About a dozen small ones of different shapes can be used to make a gay fiesta string to decorate your room, the sun porch or the rumpus room.

Allow the gourds to dry until their shells are hard. If the colors fade while drying (or if they were white gourds to begin with) you can paint them in several bright colors with enamel.

Drill small holes through the gourds near the tips where the stems were attached. Drive the drill through the shell on one side and right on through the shell on the opposite side so the holes are in line with each other. On small round gourds that have no pronounced tip, run the drill through from top to bottom.

Use bright colored pearl cotton, or thread of similar thickness, for assembling the string.

In addition to the gourds, about two dozen artificial flower leaves will be needed.

Thread a darning needle with a 36″ length of thread. Double it and tie a knot about 2″ from the end. Pass the needle through a leaf near the stem end and draw the thread through until the knot is against the leaf. Pass the needle through the holes in the gourd, then through the second leaf—photo 1. Tie the thread together at the top of the gourd. Tie a series of knots about ¼″ apart for a distance of about 2″ along the thread— photo 2. Prepare a second gourd in the same manner. Knot the strings of the two gourds together as in photo 3. Prepare a third gourd and tie its strings to the other two. Put strings on the rest of the gourds, using 24″ lengths of thread. Knot the strings above each gourd for a distance of about 1½″. Braid the strings of the first three gourds together for a distance of about 2½″ (photo 4). Lay the string of the fourth gourd along one of the strings of the braid and work it into the braid. Continue adding strings of additional gourds it intervals of 2″-3″. Photo 5 shows how one of these strings is added, close to the end of one of the first strings. When the gourds have all been added, continue the braiding to finish the hanging string. Tie the end of the braid into a loop. Photo 6 shows the completed fiesta string. You can make one any length you wish by adding more gourds.

73

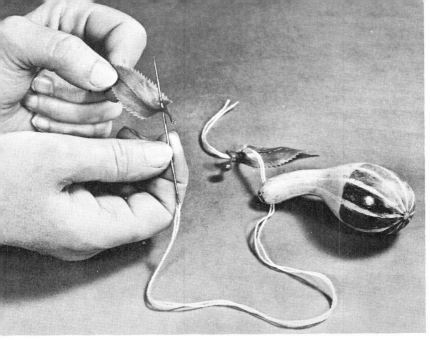

1. Drill holes through the gourds near the tip. Knot the doubled thread about 2″ from the end. Pass the needle through a leaf and push it against the knot. Then pass the needle through the gourd, then through a second leaf.

2. Bring the end of the string, below the first leaf, to the top of the gourd and tie it to the longer piece. Tie knots in the string at intervals of about 1/4″, for a distance of about 2″ along the string.

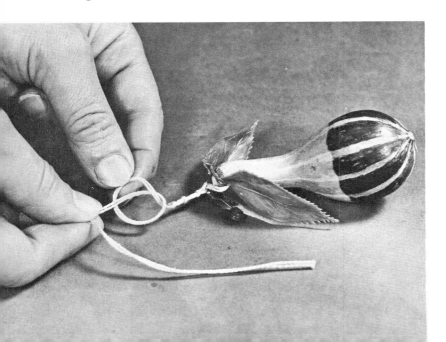

3. Prepare a second gourd as you did the first. Note that this gourd shown as number 2 is a small round one and the hole through it was drilled from bottom through the top. Here the knot is put in the end of the doubled string and drawn against the bottom of the gourd. Both leaves are strung on above the gourd. Hold the strings of the two gourds together above the knots in the individual strings, and tie them together.

4. Prepare a third gourd. Tie its string to the other two. Braid the three sets of strings together for a distance of about 2".

5.   Prepare the rest of the gourds. Add them, one at a time at intervals of 2"-3" (they should be far enough apart to hang free along the string) by laying the string alongside one of the three strands and working it into the braid.

6.   When all gourds are added, continue braiding the strands to finish the hanging string. Tie the end into a loop.

Chapter 13

FUN WITH MARBLES

One sign of spring, it is said, is a marble ring scratched in the ground wherever a group of boys get together. Marbles are popular playthings all over the world and may be made of clay, glass, stone or other materials. All sorts of games may be played with them and each country seems to have its own popular version. In Brazil most boys are seldom without a pocketful of marbles so they can play their favorite game of Gude whenever two or more boys get together. Before they begin they decide what the winner of the game will get. It may be a marble or two to be given by each loser. To play the game they dig three small holes in the ground about four feet apart in triangular formation. One of the players shoots at a hole from about a foot away. If he is successful in getting his marble into the hole, he tries for the second hole. If he misses, he must leave the marble lie where it stopped. If it has stopped directly in line with the hole, the next player has a chance to try to hit it with his own marble and knock it well out of range. Then he may shoot again for the first hole, playing his marble from where it lies.

The players go around the hole three times and the first one to do this successfully is the winner. He collects the forfeits from the other players before the next game is started.

Here are two marble games that you can make.

Chapter 14

PENNING THE PIGS

This is a giant-sized version of a pocket-sized puzzle of a type you may be familiar with. It's even more tricky than its Lilliput cousin.

You will need two cardboard box lids. One from a shoe or hosiery box or a similar kind, the other a round one from a small size cornmeal or oatmeal box. Cut away a section of the rim of the round box, about one-fifth of the circumference. Cut away the top of the round lid also to within about one-fourth inch of the edge. Spread glue on the ledge that is left and glue this "pigpen" to the inside center of the larger box lid.

Place three marbles into the box lid and time yourself to see how long it takes you to get all three "pigs" into the pen. It's not as easy as you might think. One "pig" goes in nicely without any argument. You may even get the second one in quite easily too, but by the time you have the box lid at just the right slant to drive in the third "pig" the ones that are already in the pen will quite likely sneak out of the opening and go running around outside again as contrary as real pigs.

78

1. Cut out a section of the round box lid and cut away the center of the lid also, leaving a rim about 1/4" wide. Glue the rim to the center of the larger box lid to make the "pen" for the "pigs."

2. The "pigs" are three marbles. Time yourself to see how long it takes to get all three into the pen. It's not as easy as you might think.

Chapter 15

MARBLE ROLL GAME

When you start a marble rolling from the top of the board you never know in which of the numbered bins at the bottom it will land. Since the final score depends completely on chance little children are just as apt to win as older players so this is a good game for mixed ages.

All pieces for the game board except the pegs, are cut of ¼″ plywood. The ten pegs are 1″ long pieces of ¼″ dowel. Lay out the locations of the peg holes on the board. Drill ¼″ diameter holes through the board at each of the locations. Dip the ends of the pegs into glue and push each into one of the holes, working it down until the bottoms of the pegs are flush with the bottom of the board.

Glue the marble bin section to the board at the end opposite the scoring notches. Mark each of the scoring notches with a number, 10 for one of the outer ones, 5 for each of the next two and 15 for the other outside notch.

Nail one of the long side pieces to the board, slanting the board so that it is against the top edge of the side piece at the marble bin end and against the bottom edge of the side piece at the scoring end of the board. Nail on the two end pieces and then the second side piece.

Apply two coats of shellac to the game board. After it has dried, paint the top edges and the outsides of the side and end pieces, using any color you wish.

The game may be played by any number of persons. Each player uses three marbles, starting each marble in a different one of the three bins. Each bin must be used. As the marble rolls downward it takes a zig-zag course as it strikes the pegs, and finally lands in one of the numbered bins. If the marble comes to rest against the bottom board without dropping into one of the bins, it does not count. Players roll their marbles by turns and each has three turns to make the game. Highest score wins.

MARBLE ROLL GAME

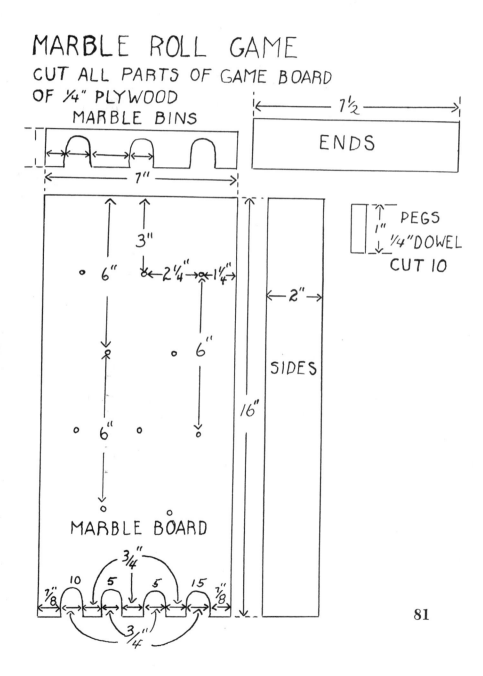

CUT ALL PARTS OF GAME BOARD
OF ¼" PLYWOOD

MARBLE BINS

ENDS

7½

7"

3"

2¼" 1¼"

6"

6"

2"

SIDES

16"

6"

6"

MARBLE BOARD

PEGS
1"
¼" DOWEL
CUT 10

10 5 5 15

¾"

¾"

⅛" ⅛"

1. Glue a peg into each of the ten holes on the board.

2. Glue and nail the marble bin strip to the end of the board opposite the scoring notches.

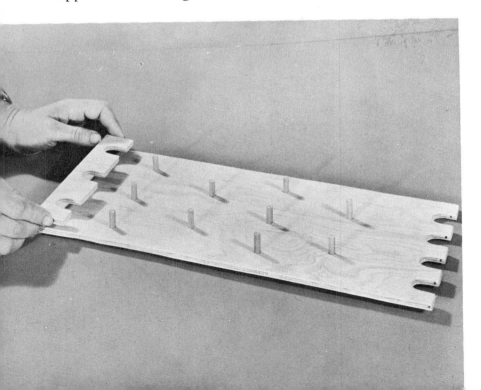

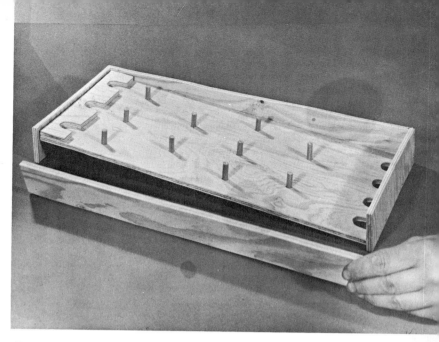

3. Nail one of the side pieces to the marble board, with the marble bin end against the upper edge of the side piece and the scoring notch end against the lower edge of the side piece.

4. To play, start a marble in one of the bins and let it roll downhill to land in one of the scoring notches. Three marbles are used and each one must be started from a different bin.

5. Since the course of the marble cannot be controlled by the players, younger ones have as good a chance to be the winner as do older players.

Chapter 16

RHYTHM INSTRUMENT
OF THE ISLANDS

People of the crescent-shaped string of Caribbean Islands are music loving folk. Their Calypso songs have a toe-tickling beat, and instruments used to accompany them are of the "rhythm" type, drums, rattles and shakers. The Calypso Carnival, the national festival held for two days before Ash Wednesday is similar to the Mardi Gras of New Orleans. The carnival is complete with masqueraders, floats and much gaiety, with always the undercurrent of the catchy music. A variety of instruments are used, drums, banjos, scraping instruments and rattles, or "Maracas" made of gourds, are shaken in pairs. Calypso music has become popular outside its place of origin to such an extent that composers have written parts for rattles into many musical scores. Suitable gourds are not always available to make rattles but you can make a tin can rattle much like a commercial Tubo which is a fine shaker with which to beat out the rhythm, accompanying other instruments or singing for your Calypso music-making sessions.

Two tall, slender cans are used. The No. 211 size is good but for a smaller instrument you may use two frozen juice cans.

Cut out one end of each can with an opener that leaves a smooth edge inside the rim.

Set the can on a piece of light weight cardboard and draw around the rim to make a "lid" just the right size to fit against the open end. Two such cardboard disks are needed, one for each can.

Cover the outsides of the cans with bright colored paper. Throw a few beans or pebbles into one can (photo 1), and a number of paper clips or tacks in the other.

Put a cardboard disk against the end of one can and wrap a strip of freezer tape (or scotch tape) around the edge of the can, leaving about half the width of the tape extending beyond the rim (photo 2).

Clip the tape at intervals of about ¼" from the edge to the rim of the can. Press the tape down on the cardboard to hold the disk firmly against the open end of the can (photo 3). Seal the end of the other can in the same manner.

Spread glue on the cardboard ends of the cans and press the two together to make the long, double Tubo (photo 4). Wrap black plastic tape around the center joint. This serves the double purpose of holding the two parts of the Tubo firmly together and adding a decorative band around the center of the instrument.

1. Drop a number of beans or pebbles into one can. Into the other drop half a dozen paper clips or tacks.

2. Hold the cardboard disk against the open end of the can. Wrap freezer tape around the can and the edge of the cardboard to hold it in place. Leave about half the width of the tape extending beyond the edge.

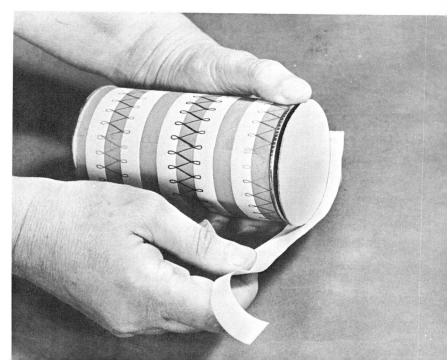

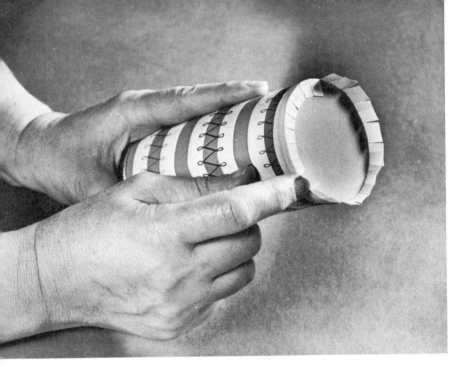

3. Snip the tape to the cardboard at intervals of about 1/4″. Stick the segment of tape down against the cardboard.

4. Glue the two cardboard ends together to make the long, double cylinder.

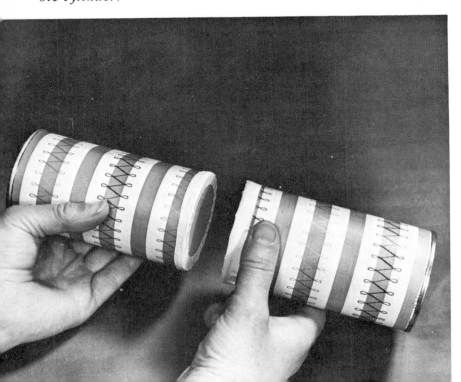

5. *Wrap plastic tape around the cylinder covering the joint. This holds the two cans firmly together and adds a decorative black band to the instrument.*

Chapter 17

GO FLY A KITE!

Who started it, this art of sending up into the air, by means of wind, those varying shapes covered with paper or cloth called kites after the fierce, soaring bird of prey—or in German, "Drache", dragon?

Legend has it that the first kite flier was Archytas, a Greek philosopher and friend of Plato, 400 years before the birth of Christ. Others say that the ancient Chinese general Hao Sin was the originator. As a matter of fact, kites were in existence long before either of these men lived. The earliest travelers in Malaya reported that natives flew large leaves and worshipped them as gods. There is evidence too, that the Egyptians flew kites centuries before Cleopatra.

Kites have been more than playthings for they have been used for all sorts of purposes. Polynesians used them for fishing. Ancient Chinese used them as signalling devices during wartime. A kite laid the first line of the bridge that now spans Niagara's gorge, and until recently the U.S. Weather Bureau sent them high into the upper air to record temperature, wind velocity and humidity. America's most famous kite flier, Benjamin Franklin, put one up in the midst of a thunderstorm in 1792 to prove that lightning was electricity. Marconi used a kite to elevate the aerial for his first transatlantic wireless telegraph-message.

Probably the people of Asia have done the most to develop the art of kite making and kite flying. They make kites in the form of all sorts of grotesque and natural creatures and some that could exist only in the wildest imagination. The Asiatic musical kite has one or more bamboo reeds on which the wind plays weird notes that can be heard for long distances. These are believed to frighten away evil spirits and are often kept flying all night high above the home.

In China kites are flown as a sign of rejoicing or in times of illness or death to drive away devils. Chinese generals have used the most terrifying kites they could think of and build to frighten away their enemies, or kites with happy faces to inspire their own armies to win a victory. In that country there is even a special day set aside in honor of kites. It is called Teng Kao, the Feast of High Flight, the day of Double Nines.

Most of us seldom think of the origin or uses but enjoy the sport on a breezy day simply for the thrill of successfully launching a colorful kite we have made and feeling its almost live tug on the string as it soars so high it is a mere speck in the blue.

Most of us have the notion, too, that a good, stiff wind is the best kind of flying weather. Nothing could be further from the truth. A steady breeze of from 8-15 mph is the most satisfactory for flying the average kite. How can you tell how strong the wind is? The Weather Bureau radio report usually gives the wind velocity but if you missed it, the following estimations, called "Beaufort's Wind Scale," will give you a good idea:

A wind of from 4-7 mph will rustle tree leaves and you can feel it lightly on your face.

8-12 mph will keep leaves in constant motion and extend a light flag.

13-18 mph tosses tree tops and blows loose paper around.

19-24 mph makes small trees sway.

Here are some general suggestions for successful kite building:

For sticks, a strong light wood with a straight grain is best. It may be soft pine, spruce, basswood or redwood. Sticks ⅜″ wide and 3/16″ thick are suitable for most kites except large ones that need heavier frames.

Covering material is usually paper such as ordinary wrapping paper. Lightweight cloth such as silk or nylon, or thin plastic material will also serve the purpose. Plastic is fastened to the framework with freezer or masking tape. Other coverings are attached by spreading glue on the top surfaces of the sticks and laying the framework onto the paper or cloth which has been smoothed out, face down, on a flat surface. Cut the paper at least ½″ larger than the kite's outline on all sides. Apply glue to this projection and lap it back around the frame or outline string.

Rigid lashing of the frame is essential. The joints may be glued and, after crossing the sticks at the desired angle, lash diagonally both ways forming an X around the sticks at the joint. Many turns of thread do a more secure job than a few turns of heavier cord.

String is needed both for building and flying the kite. For flight lines, the larger the kite the stronger the string must be. Mason's chalk line makes a satisfactory flying cord for large box kites; nylon fishing line works well for lighter weight ones.

Most kites require a tail for proper performance. It is not the weight but the bulk and surface which balances the kite, so a tail made of light weight material is the most effective. Plastic cloth or even pleated typing paper pinched in at the center to make it fan out, works well. A good tail of plastic is made of six pieces each 1½″ wide and 6″-8″ long, tied through the center to the cord at intervals of 5″-6″ apart. The stronger the wind, the more tail is needed to balance the kite. Attach the tail at the kite's lowest point.

A kite usually flies best if the bridle is at an angle of from 30 to 40 degrees from horizontal. To make the kite a high flier or floater, tilt the top forward by making the upper legs of the bridle shorter. This increases the angle of lift and decreases the wind resistance. The kite won't pull as hard but it will climb higher and float more nearly horizontal. However, if the top legs of the bridle are shortened too much the kite may tip forward and allow the wind to blow over the top, causing it to dive violently or bob up and down.

Chapter 18

MALAY BOW KITE

One of the easiest to make and a dependable flier is the Malay Bow Kite. This is a good one to begin on. Two sticks of the same length are used. They may be as long as you like but 14″ is good.

Place the crosspiece a little more than one-seventh of the distance from the top of the vertical stick. Lash the two sticks together securely.

Cut notches around the horizontal stick ¼″ from each end. Tie a piece of string securely around one end of this stick. catching it in the notch. Wrap the string around the other end, catching it in the notch. Pull the string to bow the cross arm, until the center of the string is about 2″ above the place where the two sticks are lashed together. Tie the string securely so the frame stays in its bowed shape. Cut a shallow notch across each end of the two sticks. Pass a string around the frame, catching it in the notches and tie the ends together to make the outline for putting on the cover. Cut and fit the paper covering as explained in the general suggestions. Attach the tail and a three-leg bridle to the ends of the horizontal crossarm and the bottom of the vertical stick. Tie on the flight string and the kite is ready for its maiden voyage.

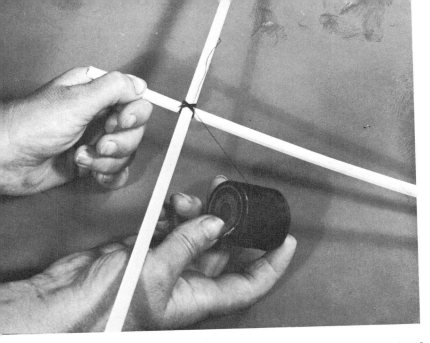

1. Use two sticks of the same length. Position the horizontal stick to cross the vertical stick about one seventh of the length of the stick down from its top. Lash the two sticks securely together by wrapping the joint with thread.

2. Tie a piece of string around one end of the horizontal stick. Wrap the string around the other end of the stick and pull it up to form the bow. Tie securely.

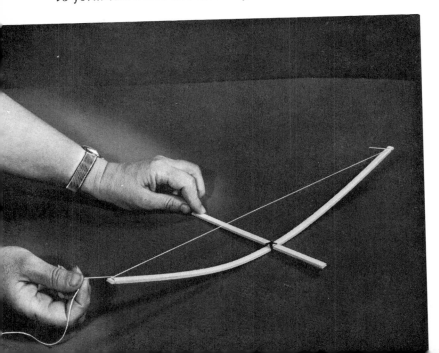

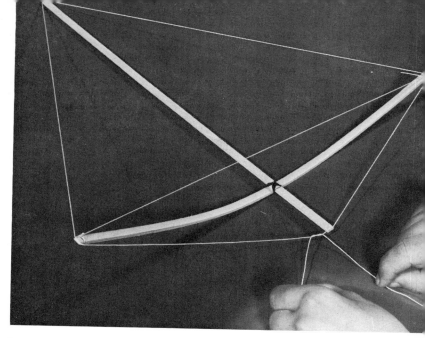

3. Catch a string in the notches at the ends of the four sticks and tie the ends securely together to make a framework for the paper covering.

4. Spread glue on the sticks and glue to the paper covering. Trim the paper at least 1/2″ larger all around than the string outline of the kite. Bring the edge of the paper around the string and glue back against itself.

Chapter 19

FLOATING HOOP KITE

This is a bit different than the others described in that strips of bamboo instead of wood are used in making the framework. A total length of 77″ is required. This is made from two 40″ lengths spliced together. Cut the strips ¼″ wide. Taper one end of each piece, the top side of one and the bottom side of the other, so they can be fitted together in a neat 3″ lap. Glue the lap and wrap it with a lashing of thread. Allow it to dry. Taper the two ends of what is now a single long strip. Roll the strip into a hoop, lap 3″, glue and lash the two ends together. Dry this joint under clamp pressure to keep it in position. Drill ⅛″ diameter holes through the frame at four points spaced equal distances apart around the circumference. Cut the bamboo pieces for the cross ribs ¼″ wide and 25″ long. Whittle each end into a ⅛″ peg. Slip the points of the pegs into the holes in the frame, bowing the strips. At the points where they cross, lash the strips securely together. Cut a circle of plastic material large enough to stretch over the frame and fold back around the hoop. Fasten the material at the four cross-stick points with masking tape. Fasten the cover at the mid-points between the cross sticks, stretching the cover smoothly over the ribs. Use strips of masking tape to complete the job of fastening the folded-back material all around the hoop. Attach the bridle and add the tail, fastening it at the same point as the bottom bridle leg.

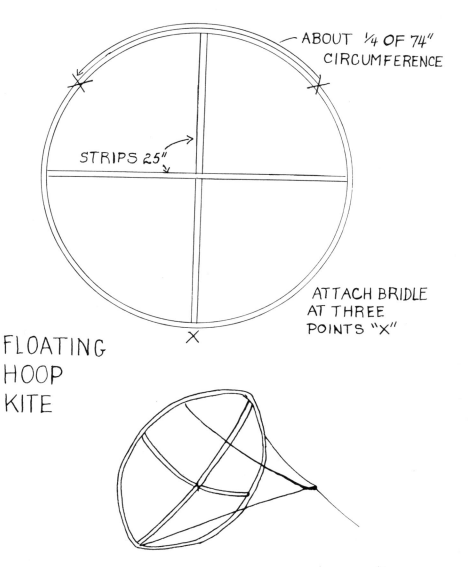

ABOUT ¼ OF 74"
CIRCUMFERENCE

STRIPS 25"

ATTACH BRIDLE
AT THREE
POINTS "X"

FLOATING
HOOP
KITE

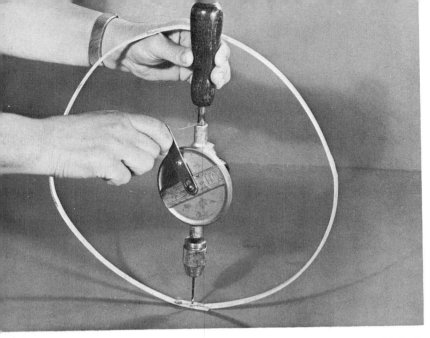

1. Form the hoop from two strips of bamboo. Drill holes through the frame at four points equally spaced around the circumference. Whittle the ends of the two cross pieces into pegs to fit into the holes.

2. Slip the pegs into place, bowing the cross pieces. Lash them together at the point where they cross each other.

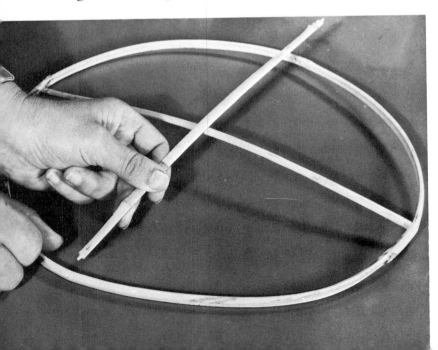

3. *Stretch the plastic covering to fit the bowed face. Bring the edge of the covering around the hoop and fasten it back against itself with short pieces of masking tape.*

4. *The hoop kite goes up easily but will not climb as high as some of the others.*

Chapter 20

PENNSYLVANIA DUTCH DESIGN APRON

"Throw papa down the stairs his hat!"
"Aunt Minnie is wonderful fat!"
"The pie is all, but the cake is yet!"
"Papa's on the table and is half et!"
"The rain makes down!" it doesn't fall.
"Comes the little red box and the train is all!"
You "Spritz the grass" . . . and "Outen the light"
And "Make the door shut" for the night.

Among the "Pennsylvania Dutch" folk who came to America before the Revolution, many customs and expressions still exist which have become known all over the country as being representative of the group of people who live in Lancaster County, Pennsylvania and its surrounding area. These people are famous for their "sayings", for certain delicious foods such as "Schnitz un knepp" and "Shoofly pie", and for the bright colored designs which they paint on their furniture, embroider on samplers, or use to decorate wall mottos, pillows, trays and many other household items.

Many of the designs use flowers and leaves, and are in many bright colors which make them especially cheery.

Pennsylvania Dutch designs are well adapted to textile stenciling. You may use this design on an apron as we have done. It would also be suitable for decorating curtains or on a luncheon cloth.

Two stencils are needed for the block design and two for the border. Copy the patterns given.

Regular stencil paper may be purchased at hobby shops where you buy your textile colors. It is quite heavy and may be used over and over. If you plan to use the stencil for only one project, it may be cut of brown wrapping paper or freezer wrap paper instead of the stencil paper.

Cut pieces of paper about 7″ square for block "A" and block "B". Trace the designs onto the paper. When block "A" is laid over block "B" the two parts of the design should line up. That is, the stems should be in their proper places in relation to the leaves and flowers, and the floral design should be centered within the border. Hold the two together against the light to be sure they are correct.

Lay a stencil on a hard surface, such as a pane of glass. Cut out the parts of the design with a razor blade, as in photo 1. Prepare all the stencils.

Unbleached muslin is a good material to use for the apron. The bright colors of the design will be very attractive on the cream colored material. If you prefer, you may use colored material, and other colors than those suggested for the stenciling. Use a strip of material 18″ wide and 30″ long for the apron. Hem the two sides and one long edge. Gather the other long edge to an 18″ long waistband. Sew on 24″ long ties. These may be either hemmed strips of muslin or ribbon. Wash the apron in warm, soapy water to remove any starch or filler. Dry and press smooth.

Lay the apron on a board padded with paper. Lay stencil block "A" in position at the center of the apron and about 4″ above the bottom edge. Hold the stencil and the cloth taut with thumbtacks to keep the cloth from creeping as you work.

Use a small pane of glass or china plate for a palette on which to mix the colors. Always add extender to the colors. This allows the paint to penetrate the fabric better, making the design more colorfast. Common toothpicks are fine for dipping colors from jars and mixing them on the palette.

Dip the brush tip lightly into the paint. Very little color is needed on the brush. Work the brush on a clean portion of the palette to push the color evenly into the bristles. Apply the color to the stencil with a "patting" motion. Work the color well into the cloth through the stencil openings for a sharp outline and even color of the design. After applying the colors on stencil "A", remove it and lay stencil "B" in place. Use only black on this one.

Stencil the design again on the right, and on the left of the center. Apply the border using the flower stencil "A" first (photo 2), then stencil "B" (photo 3).

After the stenciling is completed, allow the apron to dry for 24 hours. This is important. You are now ready to "set" the color. Lay the apron, right side up, on a piece of brown wrapping paper. Place a cloth over the design and iron for at least

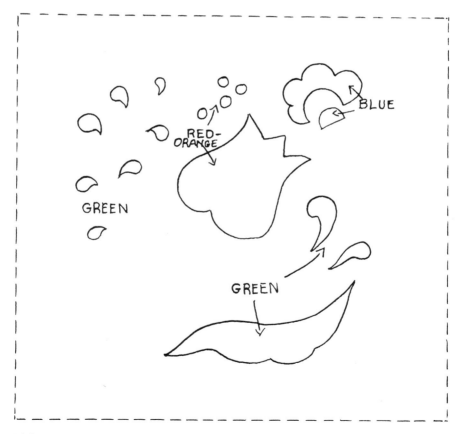

BLOCK "A"

one minute. Turn the apron face down on the paper and iron on the wrong side. If the material is rayon, iron at a cooler temperature for a longer time. After the color is set, the piece may be pressed with a damp cloth, if necessary to remove wrinkles.

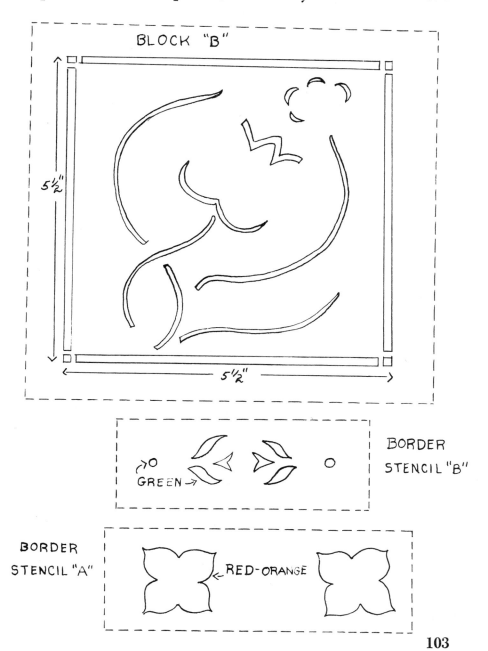

BLOCK "B"

$5\frac{1}{2}''$

$5\frac{1}{2}''$

GREEN

BORDER STENCIL "B"

BORDER STENCIL "A"

RED-ORANGE

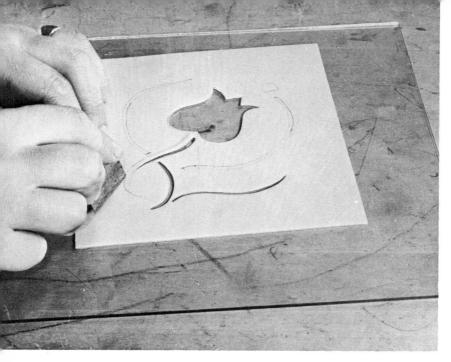

1.   Cut out the stencil with a razor blade. The edges should be clean and sharp.

2.   In applying the design, use block "A" first, then block "B". Line up block "B" so that the stems and black accents on the flowers are in their proper places. In stenciling the border, use border stencil "A" first.

3. Line up border stencil "B" so that the flower centers are in their proper places in the centers of the flowers which have already been stenciled.

4. The completed Pennsylvania Dutch design textile painted apron.

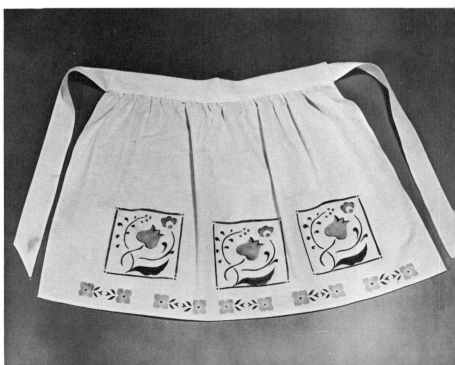

Chapter 21

BABUSHKA

This hood is easy to make and brightly gay with its Pennsylvania Dutch embroidery and felt flower appliqué design. Use wool material for the babushka and line it with coat lining material or bright red shirting flannel for extra coziness. Make the hood and the lining just the same. Cut material 9″ x 18″. Fold it in half to make a 9″ square. Seam along one edge from the fold to the bottom edge. Sew two tucks on each side to shape the bottom of the hood as indicated in the diagram. Prepare the lining in the same manner. Lay the lining and the hood with the right sides together and stitch along the front edge. Hem the ties. Turn the hood right side out and turn in the bottom edges, catching the ties between the lining and the hood.

Embroider the stem and branches design on each side of the hood, using outline stitch. Cut the flowers and leaves of felt and stitch each one in its proper place with several overcasting stitches, photo 1.

Make a yarn pompom in variegated colors matching the felt flowers, to finish off the peak of the hood. Cut two circles of light cardboard, 2″ in diameter. Cut a ¾″ circle opening in the center of each. Hold the two cardboard circles together and wrap with different colors of yarn, passing the yarn through the center opening and around the outside edge, as in photo 2. Continue wrapping, alternating the colors, until the center opening is completely closed with yarn. Snip the yarn strands around the edge (photo 3). Slip a tying cord between the two circles of cardboard (photo 4) and tie it tightly to hold the yarn strands together. Pull the cardboard circles out and sew the pompom to the tip of the hood.

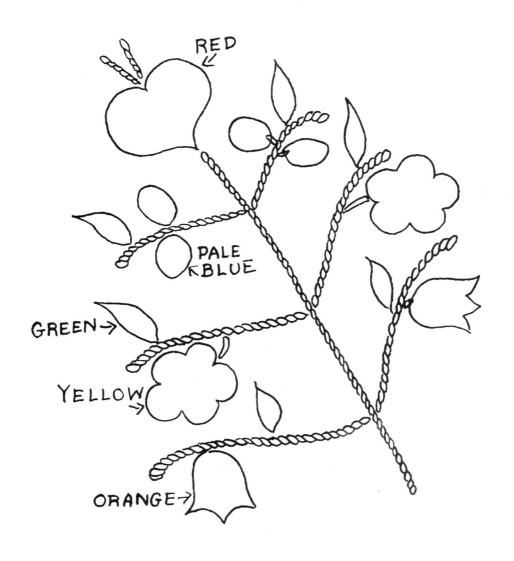

RED

PALE
BLUE

GREEN →

YELLOW →

ORANGE →

BABUSHKA DESIGN

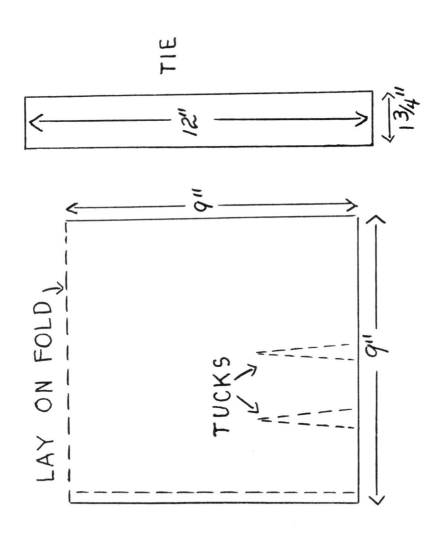

TIE

12"

1 3/4"

9"

9"

LAY ON FOLD

TUCKS

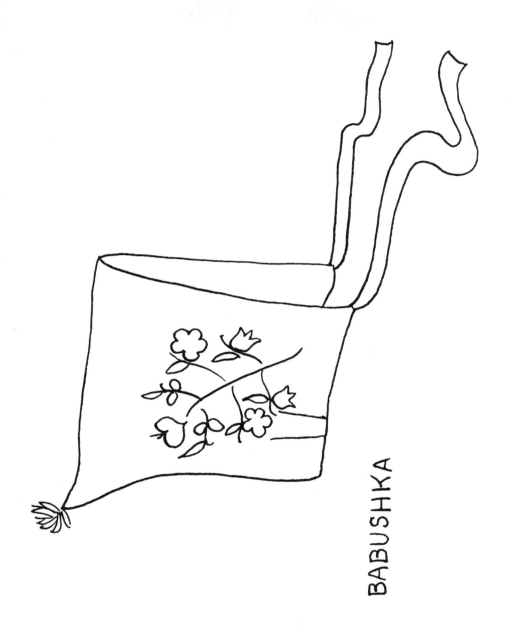

BABUSHKA

1. After finishing the cap embroider the stem and branches in green on each side. Cut the flowers and leaves of bright colored felt and fasten each in its proper position using several overcasting stitches.

2. Hold the two cardboard circles together and wind with strands of yarn in colors to match the felt flowers. Pass the yarn through the center opening and around the edge. Work around and around the circle until the center is completely filled with yarn.

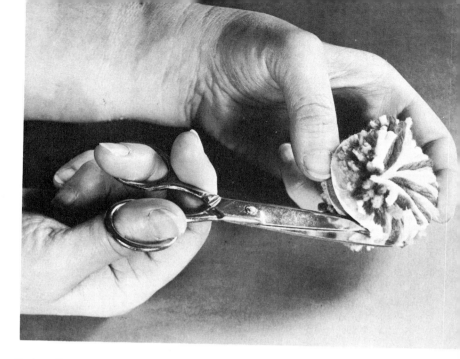

3. Snip the yarn strands where they pass around the edges of the cardboard circles.

4. Pass a tie cord between the two cardboard circles around the strands of yarn. Pull it as tight as possible and tie in a square knot. Pull out the cardboard circles and fluff out the pompom.

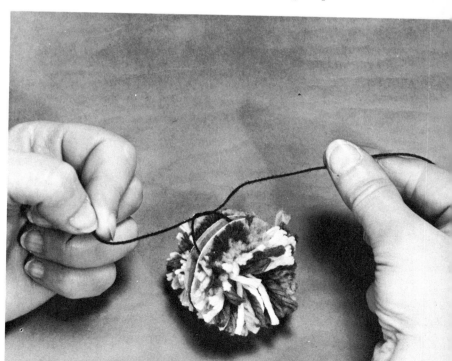

5. *The Babushka makes a cozy head covering for winter sports.*

Chapter 22

BLOCK PRINTING WITH ERASER STAMPS

The art of hand block printing to decorate cloth was known to the Chinese, the Egyptians, and the Romans, but it is believed to have originated with the people of India. There can be little doubt that it was from this country that the knowledge of the craft spread to Europe by way of Persia, Asia Minor and the Levant. During the Middle Ages, monks in some of the monasteries in Germany made beautiful hand-blocked linens and there are still a few examples of these to be seen in museums. Then, for some reason, the art of hand block printing seems to have died out and its secrets were lost in Europe. In India, however, hand printed textiles continued to be produced. Traders brought samples of the materials to England again early in the sixteenth century and the craft was revived. Eventually India Prints found their way to the New World also. They were so much admired that print works were established to produce printed cloth in imitation of the Indian fabrics. The first was set up in what is now known as old Deer Park, Richmond, in 1690, but it was not until about a century later that the printing of textiles really became a thriving business. In 1783 a Scotsman named Bell invented a cylinder printing machine. This made it possible to print cloth much faster and more accurately. As a result printed fabrics were less expensive. The same type of machine is still used. However, the art of hand printing has not again been lost and hand blocked textiles are available in more expensive fabrics.

The first blocks were of wood with the design left in relief and the surface between the lines cut away, or else the design itself was gouged out and the part of the block around it did the printing while the design remained the color of the cloth. Linoleum blocks too, have been used. Perhaps one of the easiest ways to make a block or stamp for printing is to cut the design on one of the surfaces of an ordinary eraser. Though the blocks are limited to the size of the eraser, they are easy to make and work very well to produce designs on cloth or paper. You can print luncheon cloths, place mats, head scarves, handkerchiefs and all sorts of other small items. You can also use the blocks to print gift papers, cover papers for waste baskets, book jackets or any number of other things. If you print on cloth, use textile paints to produce a washable fabric. On paper you can use hobby enamels, printer's ink or tempera paints.

Make the blocks of either "soap" or "artgum" erasers. They seem to work equally well. One eraser can be used to make several stamps. It may be cut into pieces to make stamps for small parts such as leaves or stems. You may carve a design into each face of the eraser.

Plan the design first on paper. If you lay the eraser on paper and draw around its outline it is easier to get the size of the design right to fit the eraser. However, if the design includes any letters they must be drawn backwards in order to print correctly.

Transfer the design to the face of the eraser. You may either sketch it on freehand or cut out the paper pattern and draw around the outline. Make a straight up and down cut all around the outline of the design, using the point of a sharp knife and making the cut about ⅛" deep. Cut away the background leaving the design in relief about ⅛" high. Be sure the edges of the design are a sharp, clean cut. The design in photo 1 shows a

114

flower and leaf all on the same stamp. This is for a one-color print. If the design is to be in several colors it is better to cut a stamp for each part, that is, one stamp having only the flower on it, another for the stem and a third for the leaf. Another advantage in having several stamps is that the design can be arranged in a number of different ways.

The simplest way to apply the paint to these small stamps is to put it on with a camel's hair brush. Apply an even coat of paint to the raised surface of the design. Be careful not to let the paint run over the edge. Place the stamp face down on the material to be printed and apply a firm, even pressure. If you don't press hard enough, the design will not print evenly. If you press too hard the paint will work beyond the edge and the design will be smudgy instead of crisp and clean. It is best to do a bit of practicing first before beginning on the piece to be printed. You will soon get the "feel" of using the eraser block. Photo 2 shows a place mat partly finished and the three blocks used in producing the border design. In making the border the center part of the design is put on first. This makes it easier to space the rest of the border correctly.

In photo 4 a test print has been made. Notice that the letters on the block are in reverse.

Some blocks can be used to make a variety of different designs depending on the way they are arranged when printing. The test strip in photo 4 shows a number of different designs that were produced by a single block. Still other arrangements could be made.

After you finish printing, clean the block with paint thinner or solvent recommended for whatever type of paint you have used, then wash the block in soap and water. They can be used over and over again.

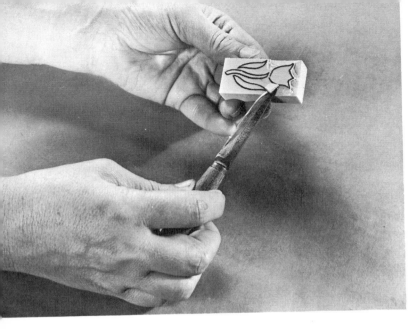

1. Lay out the design on the eraser. Cut straight down all around the outline of the design to a depth of approximately 1/8". Cut away the eraser around the design so that it stands up in relief about 1/8" above the background. Be sure the edges are clean and sharp.

2. Apply the paint to the surface of the design, then stamp the design onto the piece to be decorated using firm, even pressure. The three stamps, arranged in different ways, are used to make the center portion and the rest of the border.

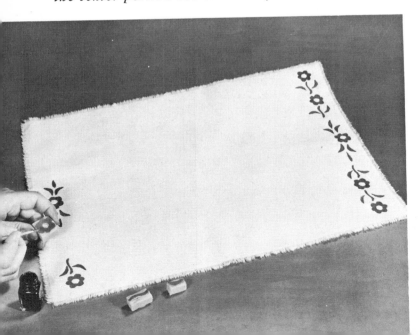

3. *If letters or numbers are a part of the design they must be backwards on the stamp to print correctly.*

4. *A single stamp can be used to produce a variety of different designs depending on the way it is arranged when printing. The test strip shows three different designs produced by the stamp. Many more arrangements would be possible.*

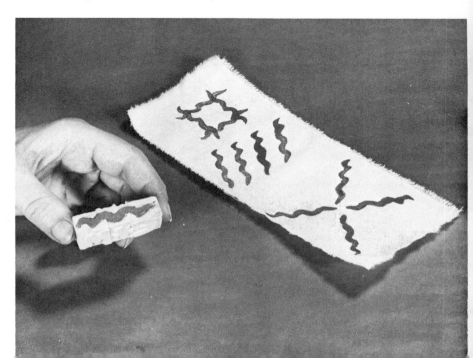

5. *A place mat decorated with an eraser stamp block print border.*

Chapter 23

MOSAICS

The putting together of many small pieces of marble, glass, tile, enamel or other materials to make patterns or pictures is known as mosaic. It is believed to be the oldest of the crafts developed by man. Some examples have been found that go back as far as 3500 B.C. The Egyptians, the first to lay mosaics, used geometric designs to decorate walls, columns and floors. The Romans later added bits of colored glass to brighten up the marble mosaics. Instead of using only geometric designs they assembled the mosaics into pictures. One of the more unusual ones showed in detail the battle of Issus. One design that was used to decorate vestibule floors was the silhouette of a dog with the inscription "cave canem" ("beware of the dog").

In the churches of Italy, where the craft of mosaics was probably the most highly developed, great artists used mosaics to make detailed pictures of the saints of the church or the Holy Family. Some of the world's most beautiful pictures are in mosaic. In St. Peter's in Rome one such picture took ten men nine years to complete. Some are made in marble only in natural colors with no paint. Gold leaf was added to others.

Then, for many years, mosaics almost disappeared except in Mexico and South America where they were used to decorate buildings and market places. In recent years they have again become popular and in addition to being used to decorate walls and buildings, to "paint" large murals, small ceramic tiles are used to make all sorts of mosaic craft items. Perhaps you have used them to decorate tray or tea tiles.

Two methods are used in applying mosaics to walls or other large surfaces. In one, the pieces to make the design are glued directly to the wall. The other is to make a full size outline drawing on heavy paper. The design on the paper is in reverse of the way it will be on the wall. The pieces are glued to the paper, face down. The paper is then cut into pieces that are small enough to be easily handled. The surface of the wall to be decorated is coated with a special cement, and into the fresh cement the pieces of the design are pressed, still with the faces glued to the original drawing which is fitted together like a jigsaw puzzle. When the cement is set the paper is torn off and the joints· packed with cement. The entire surface is then cleaned.

Mosaic for floors is popular in our day wherever an easily cleaned surface is wanted, on the floors of public buildings, in swimming pools or even in the kitchens or bathrooms of homes.

POPCORN MOSAIC

This is a different type of mosaic in which you can really use your imagination to make all sorts of colorful pictures. The mosaic pieces are unpopped popcorn kernels. They are dyed, then glued to a sandpaper background and mounted in a picture frame without glass.

Get a bag of white popcorn and soak the kernels in a solution of food coloring and water. The more concentrated the solution, the deeper the colors will be. We used red, yellow, blue, green colors plus the natural white ones, in this design. Mix about half a cupful of dye solution in each color. Pour the kernels into the solution and allow them to soak until the desired color is reached. If they have soaked for several hours and the color seems too pale you may need to add more food coloring and stir. Spread the dyed kernels on paper to dry before using them.

Cut a piece of plywood to fit an 8″ x 10″ frame. Glue on a sheet of coarse sandpaper and dry under weight to make a tight, all-over bond of the sandpaper to the wood.

Draw the design for your mosaic picture to fit the background. Cut out the picture in outline and lay it on the sandpaper. Draw around the outline, then fill in the rest of the design free hand.

Glue the kernels, one at a time, to the background to fill in the picture area, working with one part of the design at a time.

You may copy this sleepy Mexican or make up your own. This picture has green cactus with white spines, which are made by using the undyed kernels glued on with their points sticking up. The Mexican wears a yellow hat with red decorations, a red shirt, blue trousers with a red stripe, white shoes and a striped serape.

121

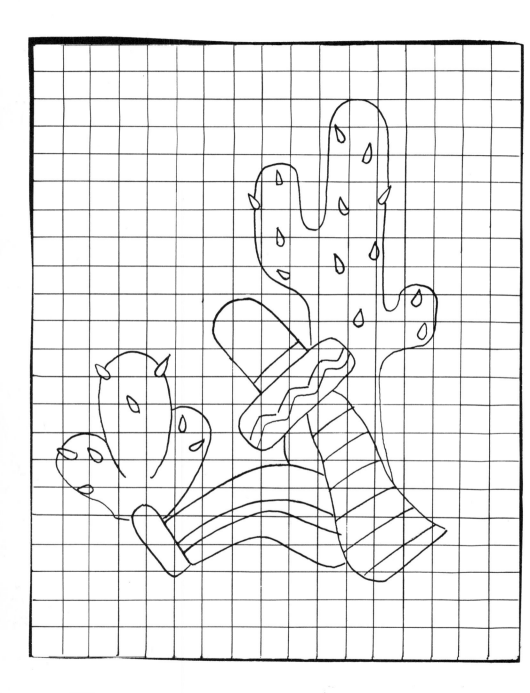

1. *Draw the design to fit the sandpaper background. Cut it out in outline and lay it on the sandpaper. Draw around the outline.*

2. *Draw the rest of the lines of the design free hand. These lines are the guides for filling in with popcorn kernels.*

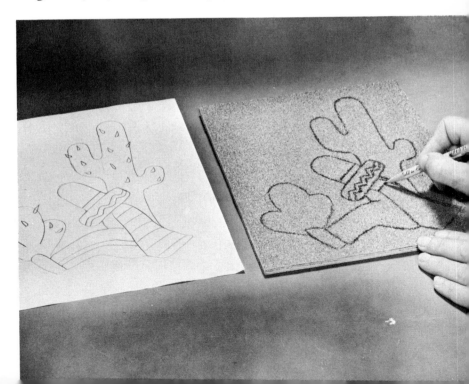

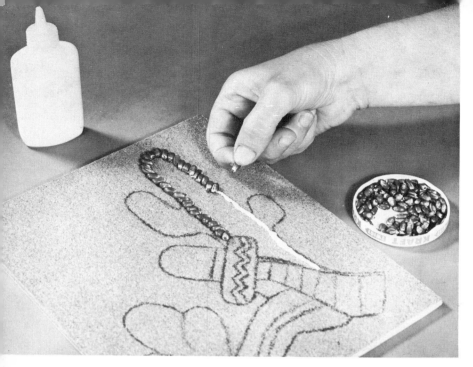

3.   Run a line of glue around the outer edge of one part of the design. Lay the kernels on the glue with the points inward.

4.   Fill in the rest of the portion of the design laying the kernels so that the points do not show. Use undyed white kernels glued in with the points sticking up to make the cactus spines.

5. *Use a frame without glass to mount your popcorn mosaic.*

Chapter 24

FROM CAN TO CANISTER

Another interesting mosaic project is making a canister from an empty can. Ceramic or vinyl tile, available in hobby shops, is glued to the cover and the can itself is wrapped with crepe paper rope. The canister illustrated is for sugar but it could be used for cookies, tea or anything else if it had a different label. A three-pound shortening can that is opened by a metal key is a good can to use.

Remove the lid from the can by wiggling it back and forth until the bit of metal that holds the two together breaks. Smooth off any roughness of metal with a fine file until there are no sharp edges left. Punch or drill a hole ⅛″ in diameter through the center of the lid.

Cover the can with a wrapping of crepe paper rope. This one has a band of brown at the top and the bottom with yellow around the rest of the can. The letters are in brown.

To make the rope, cut through a fold of crepe paper 1″ from the end, across the grain. Stretch and pull the strip through a crepe paper twister. If you have no twister, fasten one end of the strip to something solid. Stretch and twist the paper by hand.

Glue one end of the strip against the bottom rim of the can. Spread glue around the can for a width of about 1″. Wrap the strip around and around the can, pushing each row down tight against the one before it so that none of the metal shows between the rows of rope. Wrap as high as the glue has been applied, then spread on another width of glue and continue wrapping. Cover the entire can to the top, as in photo 1.

Chapter 25

JAPANESE SCROLL PAINTING

Japanese painting really originated in China, but it is a mistaken idea that the Japanese are merely imitators in the field of art. Though it is true that the great Chinese empire did influence the smaller island nation, just as Italy and Greece influenced Western Europe, the Japanese developed a technique in painting and the making of prints which is distinctly their own.

Japanese painting uses a symbolic, rather than a natural representation, and does not add any of the shadows which we see when looking at an object. A complete scene, with all the details, is not painted, but only those parts which are considered to be the most important, with blank spaces between them for emphasis. Because of this, the paintings or prints seem to us to have a "flat" appearance, but they are very striking and attractive. The painting is not done from models, or by looking at a scene and painting what is before the eye of the artist. Instead they try to train the mind and the eye by studying closely whatever is to be used in the design, then painting "from memory."

Chinese inks or water colors are usually used. Sometimes rice paste or a diluted fish glue is added to the colors. The painting is done mostly on silk or absorbent paper. Very definite strokes, similar to those used in Japanese brush writing, make leaves, flowers, or other parts of the design when this type of stroke is practical.

Pictures are often in the form of hanging paintings, called "Kakemono." These are long scrolls mounted on fine brocade, and are kept rolled up except when they are on display. Then they are hung in a special alcove, the "Tokonoma," used only for showing the scroll pictures. There are also horizontal scrolls, called "Makinoma," which may be very long, and tell a picture story of some battle or scene from Japanese life. Some of the finest examples of painting are done on folding screens. These are often in color on a gold or silver background and are very rich looking.

A Japanese-type wall scroll is an interesting painting project. Good background material is a piece cut from an inexpensive paper window shade. Hardware or variety stores carry such shades without the rollers. Paper may be used instead but it will not be as durable. The scroll illustrated is 12 inches wide and 24 inches long. You may make it any size, keeping those proportions.

Enlarge the pattern by laying out 1-inch squares on paper. Draw into each square the part of the design which appears in the corresponding smaller square of the pattern diagram. The numbers on the diagram are a color guide only and need not be copied. Transfer the finished pattern to the scroll material.

Use water colors or tempera paints to fill in the parts of the design. Paint first all of the areas that are white. Next paint all the areas that are light gray, then those that are tan, and so on, using a darker color each time and finishing with the black areas.

Cut four pieces of wood for the ends of the scroll, each piece measuring ¾ inch wide, 14 inches long, and ⅜ inch thick. Sandpaper the wood thoroughly. Paint each piece black on the ends and three sides, leaving one ¾ inch wide side unpainted.

Glue the bottom of the scroll to the unpainted side of one piece of wood. Glue on the second piece of wood, with the scroll material sandwiched between the two.

Use bright colored pearl cotton or similar heavy thread as a wrapping around the ends of the stick. Spread glue on the wood and begin the wrapping close against the edge of the scroll. Continue wrapping to within ¼ inch of the outer end. Push the turns tight against each other so no black wood shows through. Clip the thread and glue down the end.

Glue a piece of wood to the bottom side of the top end of the scroll. Before gluing on the second piece of wood, sandwich the hanging cord between the two pieces as shown in photo 5. Leave about 5 feet of the cord free before laying it across the wood. After gluing down the second wood strip, wrap the cord around the ends of the stick as you did at the bottom.

If you wish to design your own, you can get additional ideas by looking at real Japanese scrolls or pictures of them which you may find in the encyclopedia or in art books at your library.

1 - WHITE
2 - LT. GRAY
3 - MED. GRAY
4 - BLACK
5 - BLUE
6 - GREEN
7 - RED
8 - TAN
9 - BROWN

134

1. *Paint all the parts of the design that are one color. Begin with white, then light gray, and so on, working from the lighter to the darker colors, finishing with black.*

2. *Paint the grasses with one brush stroke for each blade. The bridge rails and the little reflection markings are black.*

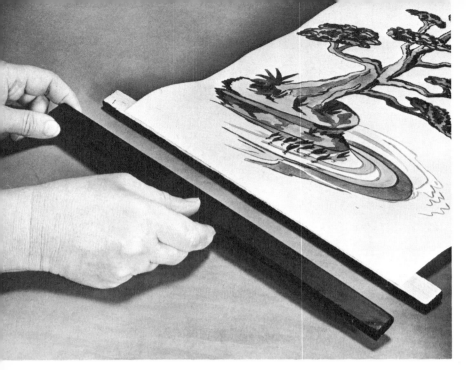

3. Sandwich the bottom end of the scroll between two strips of wood that have been painted black.

4. Wrap the ends of the wood strips with heavy thread. Begin the wrapping close against the scroll and wrap to within 1/4 inch of the outer end.

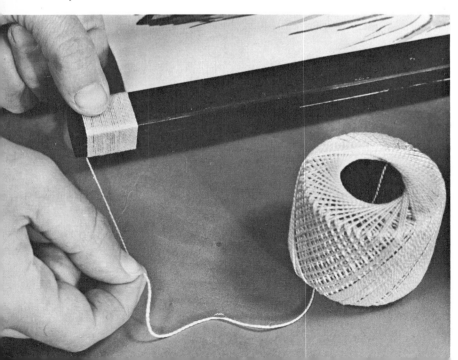

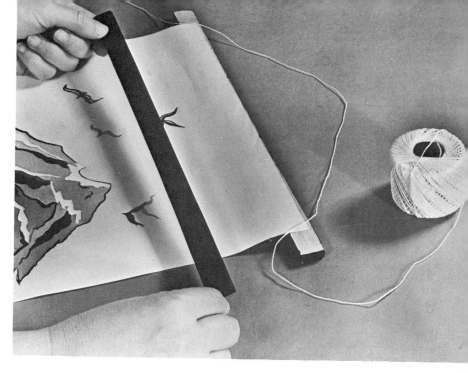

5. *Sandwich the hanging cord, at the top end, between the two wood strips, then wrap the cord around the ends as you did at the bottom.*

6. *The completed "Kakemono."*

Chapter 26

MULTIPLYING PEEP BOX

In England, many years ago, Peep Shows were a popular form of entertainment. Traveling showmen carried little houses or stages on their backs from place to place. Whenever he could find an audience the showman set up the apparatus on a little platform. People would pay a small fee to peek through the holes in the front to see the scene set up inside. At a time when there were no movies or TV and little other entertainment, these shows were popular and some of them were very elaborate. One favorite had a single picture at the back which was a lithograph of the center hall of Prince Albert's Museum. In ordinary light the viewer would see the great hall with lights shining through tiny holes which appeared to be the lighted candles of the hanging chandeliers. Then, when a light was turned on at the back of the picture it would entirely change and the many tiny lights seemed to be coming, not from the chandeliers, but from the tower of London.

Just as puzzling and intriguing was another type of peep box called "Multum in Provo" which might be translated as "A multitude in a small place." Inside the box there seemed to be so many figures that it seemed impossible so great a number could be crowded in so small a space. Actually, it was done with mirrors. There were only several figures inside the box but they were made to look like a great many by means of the mirror lining.

A miniature "Multum" is fun to make and an interesting novelty to puzzle your friends. Pocket mirrors measuring 2″ x 3″ are a good size to use. They are available in dime stores. Four of them will be needed.

Make a small cardboard box to fit the mirrors. Three sides of the box should be ¼″ higher than the width of the mirrors and all four sides of the box should each be ⅛″ longer than the length of the mirrors. The fourth side of the box should be just as high as the width of the mirrors.

Fold up the three taller sides of the box and tape them together, leave the lower side of the box open for the present.

Cut a piece of ¼″ thick wood to snugly fit the bottom of the box on the three sides that are taped together, but leave a "crack" the same width as the thickness of the mirrors at the front end. Cover one side of the piece of wood with colored paper, then glue the wood to the bottom of the box.

Glue mirrors to the three sides of the box that are taped together. Arrange small figures on the "floor" and when the arrangement is satisfactory, glue the figures to the base. Glue the fourth mirror to the front of the box and tape together the last two corners to complete the box. This mirror should fit against the bottom of the box in the "crack" between the base and the front side.

Cut a cover of translucent white plastic to fit the top of the box, to let the light through for viewing the scene inside. If white plastic is not easily available, you may use clear sheet plastic and "frost" it by rubbing it with fine sandpaper, or you may cover the top of the box with white tissue paper. This is a perfectly satisfactory cover, as far as transmitting light is concerned, though of course it is not as strong.

Now look into the box through the narrow slot across the front. No matter from which angle you look, there seem to be many little figures inside instead of just the few you put in. As the box is brought close to the eyes, you see only the reflections and not the figures inside so it is quite a puzzle to folks who do not know how it was made.

1. If you are using 2″ × 3″ mirrors, the bottom of the box should measure 2 1/8″ × 3 1/8″, three of the sides measure 2 1/4″ × 3 1/8″ and the fourth side measures 2″ × 3 1/8″. If mirrors of a different size are used the dimensions will need to be adjusted accordingly. Make the box of light weight cardboard. Tape the three taller sides together at the corners. Leave the short side open for the present.

2. Cut a piece of 1/4″ thick wood to 3 1/8″ × 3 1/16″ size. Cover one side with colored paper and glue the wood to the inside bottom of the box. It should be a tight fit against the three sides that have been taped together, with a 1/16″ "crack" at the front end.

3. *Glue three mirrors inside the box against the three sides of the box that are taped together.*

4. *Arrange three or four tiny figures inside the box. When the arrangement satisfies you, glue the figures to the base.*

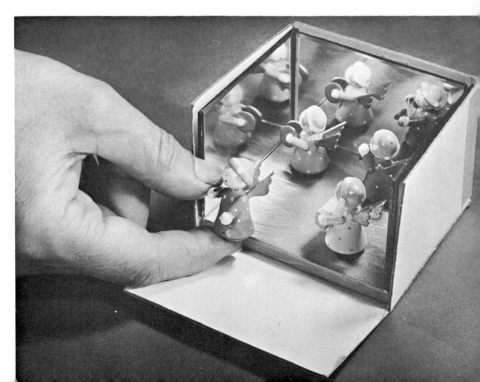

5. Glue the fourth mirror to the front of the box, then tape together the corners to complete the box. The front mirror fits against the bottom of the box in the "crack" left by the wood base, so that the front side of the box and its mirror is 1/4" lower than the other three sides.

6. When the box is completed the few little figures will be reflected by the mirrors on all sides making them appear to be many instead of few enclosed in the small space.

7.   Cut a lid for the box from translucent white plastic. Or substitute a cover of white tissue paper which is equally effective though not as strong. Glue the lid in place.

8.   When you look through the narrow slot between the front side and the cover of the box, you will see many little figures. No matter from which angle you look, there are so many inside you cannot count them all. As you bring your eye close to the slot you will see only the reflections and not the actual figures.

Date Due